GOLDEN MENGARIS TREES ALONG A RIVER BANK

THUNDER CLOUD BACKED BY THE SHADOW OF A CIRRUS CLOUD

TIME
LIFE
BOOKS

LIFE NATURE LIBRARY
LIFE SCIENCE LIBRARY
GREAT AGES OF MAN
FOODS OF THE WORLD
TIME-LIFE LIBRARY OF ART
LIFE LIBRARY OF PHOTOGRAPHY
THE EMERGENCE OF MAN
THE OLD WEST
THE ART OF SEWING

BORNEO

THE WORLD'S WILD PLACES/TIME-LIFE BOOKS/AMSTERDAM

BY JOHN MACKINNON
AND THE EDITORS OF TIME-LIFE BOOKS

THE WORLD'S WILD PLACES

European Editor: Dale Brown
Editorial Staff for *Borneo*:
EDITOR: John Man
Deputy Editor: Simon Rigge
Picture Editor: Pamela Marke
Design Consultant: Louis Klein
Staff Writers: Michael Brown, Mally Cox,
Dan Freeman, Heather Sherlock
Art Director: Graham Davis
Assistant Art Director: Roy Williams
Design Assistant: Joyce Mason
Picture Researchers:
Kerry Arnold, Margrite Prah
Picture Assistant: Cathy Doxat-Pratt
Editorial Co-ordinator: Jackie Matthews
Copy Staff: Julia West

Consultants
Botany: Christopher Grey-Wilson, Phyllis Edwards
Geology: Dr. Peter Stubbs
Herpetology: David Ball
Ichthyology: Dr. Alwyne Wheeler
Invertebrates: Michael Tweedie
Ornithology: I. J. Ferguson-Lees
Zoology: Dr. P. J. K. Burton

The captions and text of the picture essays were
written by the staff of Time-Life Books.

Valuable assistance was given in the preparation of
this volume by the Time-Life correspondent in
Singapore, Mike Pitt.

ISBN 7054 0099 9

The Authors:
John MacKinnon has sustained his interest in Borneo since his undergraduate days at Oxford, when he spent four months in Sabah on an expedition to study orang-utans. He has been back several times since, including one year living in the jungle, and his studies there have been the subject of two BBC films. Besides numerous scientific papers, he has published *Animals of Asia* and *In Search of the Red Ape*.

David Attenborough wrote the Nature Walk and gave valuable assistance on other parts of this book. Widely known in Britain for his television programmes on natural history subjects, he has been to Borneo three times for the BBC. On his latest expedition he fulfilled an old ambition to climb Mount Kinabalu, the subject of his Nature Walk.

The Consultant:
Paul Richards has conducted research in many of the tropical rain forests of the Old and New Worlds, and his book, *The Tropical Rain Forest*, is an outstanding general work on the subject. He spent five months in Sarawak in 1932 and has twice visited Borneo since. He is now Professor of Botany at the University College of North Wales in Bangor.

The Cover: On the side of a wet, mist-laden valley, the Bornean jungle is a tangle of lush foliage, tall hardwoods hung with a bedraggled rigging of creepers and set off by the occasional giant tree fern. Only in the few places where gaps occur in the leafy screen does sunlight relieve the secretive gloom of the island's tropical rain forest.

Contents

Hills and Forests, Rivers and Swamps

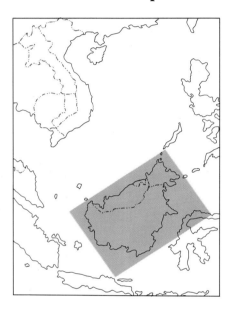

The rain-forested island of Borneo, lying within the green rectangle on the outline map above, is the largest island in the Malay archipelago and the third largest in the world. Borneo is 830 miles long and 600 miles wide, and is divided politically into Sabah and Sarawak, which belong to the Federation of Malaysia; Brunei, a tiny British protectorate; and the largest portion, Kalimantan, which is part of Indonesia. The island lies astride the Equator, directly in the path of rain-bringing winds. Tropical forests extend from the coastal areas (dark green shading), through the hilly lowlands between 600 and 3,000 feet (light green), and over the central highlands which rise above 3,000 feet (yellow). A maze of rivers drain away the torrential rains; and extensive swamps, indicated by feathery tufts, sustain the mangroves and other water-tolerant trees that give the island a dark-green fringe.

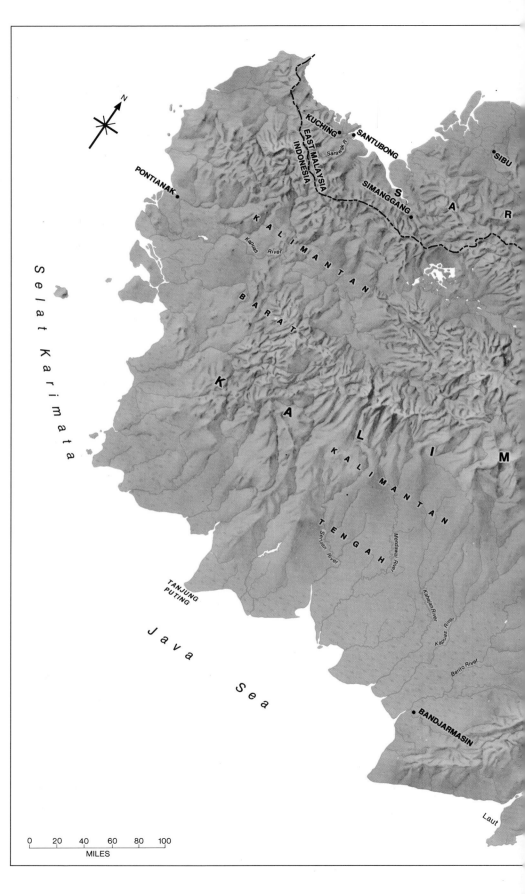

South China Sea

Sulu Sea

Celebes Sea

Makassar Strait

Teluk Tomini

MIRI
SERIA
BRUNEI
VICTORIA
Labuan
KOTA KINABALU
PAPAR
KUDAT
SENAJA
BANDAU

BRUNEI
Brunei Bay
CROCKER RANGE
Mt. Kinabalu
13,455 ft.
SABAH
KLAGAN

Niah Cave
Niah River
Padas River
Mt. Trus Madi
8,134 ft.
SEPILOK
SANDAKAN

Baram River
Gomanton Cave
Kinabatangan River

S A R A W A K
Rajang River
USUN APAU PLATEAU
KELABIT HIGHLANDS
BRASSEY RANGE
Tapadong Cave
Segama River

HOSE MOUNTAINS
EAST MALAYSIA
INDONESIA
Bole River
Batu Balus Cave
LAHAD DATU

Mentarang River
TAWAU
Darvel Bay

K A L I M A N T A N
Kayan River
TARAKAN

T I M U R
Kayan River

Mahakam River

TALOK

SAMARINDA

KALIMANTAN SELATAN
BALIKPAPAN

TOMPO

SULAWESI (CELEBES)

DONGGALA

PALU

PARIGI

1/ The Jungle Island

Thus it is that in the warm and moist and equable climate of the tropics, each available station is seized upon, and becomes the means of developing new forms of life especially adapted to occupy it. ALFRED RUSSEL WALLACE/ *THE MALAY ARCHIPELAGO*

The aircraft came in low over the South China Sea, and I caught my first glimpse of Borneo, the vast tropical island that was to be my home for many months. Beyond the shore, thousands of square miles of green jungle stretched unbroken far to the south, one of the largest expanses of tropical rain forest outside South America. Our air route followed the western coastline, and below I could see clusters of stilted houses on the mudflats and the neat white sails of fishing boats that explored the shallows. Between the villages stretched the dark green coastal fringe of the mangrove swamps, interrupted occasionally by narrow streams winding their way to the warm sea.

We left the coast and flew inland. An undulating carpet of tall rain forest passed beneath us, an elaborate pattern of the crowns of thousands of trees. A hundred shades of green blended to form a continuous layer of leafy canopy, rising and falling with the hills and valleys, softening the hidden contours of rock and soil. Borneo, the third biggest island in the world, is still largely covered in forest. The trees reach up and over the very peaks of the long mountainous backbone of the island. Great rivers drain these remote highlands and then meander through the equally dense forests of the lowland alluvial plains.

We turned north and crossed the Baram river which twisted down its broad valley through the hills. Close to the water a cluster of tin roofs flashed in the sunlight, and a patchwork of tiny fields and clearings showed where the edges of the jungle had been cut back. At the junction of a small tributary stood a Dyak long-house—home for a whole village gathered beneath a single roof. A fleet of *sampan*, each with a palm thatch roof, was drawn up in neat rows on the beach. Almost certainly there would be barking dogs and cackling chickens, children splashing in the shallows, the smell of wood smoke in the long-house, and old men swapping tales, grinning with rotten, betel-blackened teeth. I could see only tiny dots, but soon I was to know and appreciate the friendly atmosphere of the riverside villages.

Behind the beach and the long-house was the jungle once more, the massed phalanx of trees constantly ready to envelop the puny clearings. Beyond the river there was no sign of human influence. Here and there a splash of white broke through the green, where sharp limestone outcrops towered through the surrounding canopy; but many of these pillars, too, were capped in trees. Only one peak in the whole of Borneo rises clear above the tree line—the bare granite summit of Mount Kinabalu. It was the jagged rampart of this great mountain that I could see silhouetted against the evening sky as our aircraft circled to land. We were approaching Kota Kinabalu, the capital of Sabah, or North Borneo as it used to be known under British rule.

In many parts of Sabah, as elsewhere in Borneo, logging companies are extracting a wealth of high quality timber, leaving a barren, devastated landscape which is soon clothed in a tangle of second-growth jungle. But there are still large areas of virgin rain forest intact. These sustain an ecological community of plants and animals which has developed over millions of years to an exceptionally high degree of diversity. It was in one of these untouched areas, far up the Segama river in eastern Sabah, that I was to spend most of my time in Borneo.

Thirty million years ago there was no rain forest, not even any land, where Borneo now lies. Water covered almost all the region occupied by the Malay archipelago. It was not until 15 million years ago that the island began to emerge from the sea, rising as extreme buckling and folding occurred in the earth's crust. Borneo is thus very young in geological time, for already the age of dinosaurs was long past. The mammals dominated life on the mainland and most of the animals in Asia would have been familiar to a modern naturalist had he taken a trip back in time. Primitive elephants, rhinoceroses, pigs and monkeys were common in the forests; early horses, antelopes, hyaenas and giraffes inhabited the savannahs. At this stage, however, the fauna of Borneo itself must have been comparatively meagre, because the island was separated from the mainland communities of animals by the sea.

During the Pliocene, between two and ten million years ago, Borneo continued to change. Gradually the sedimentary deposits of which it consisted—sandstone, mudstone and occasional layers of dolomitic limestone which had lain at the bottom of the Bornean sea—were raised by constant tectonic movements to form the main mountain chains. At the same time, dramatic geological events were taking place in the unstable zone encircling the island. The mountains of Sumatra, Java, the Philippines, Sulawesi (formerly Celebes) and the Lesser Sunda Islands were rising to the accompaniment of intense volcanic activity. Borneo, however, lay just off this "belt of fire" and escaped relatively unscarred. The only features of volcanic origin today are the Hose mountains and a few small volcanic cones along the eastern coast of what is now Sabah. One really large-scale geological happening in Borneo was the rise of Mount Kinabalu in the north of the island, which pushed its way up as a great igneous mass through the overlying sedimentary rocks.

Just as Borneo escaped many of the major upheavals of the Pliocene, so, too, it was little disturbed by the climatic swings of the Pleistocene. The last two million years on this planet have been dramatically unstable. Four times the polar ice caps expanded and great glaciers scoured the temperate regions of the world. During the glaciations, rain was scarce over much of the world and the savannah extended as far south as the Malay peninsula. But in Borneo there seem to have been no drastic changes in rainfall and the island's natural thick forest has survived with little change.

However, there was one very important effect that stemmed from the expansion of the ice caps. So much water was locked up in ice that the world sea level dropped. The water around Borneo was very shallow— as it is today—and when the oceans contracted, the island was connected by dry land to the rest of Asia. So, too, were Sumatra and Java, and the three islands joined up to form one vast expanse of tropical rain forest covering an area known as Sundaland.

Once this land bridge had been formed, Borneo came into direct contact with Asia and its own fauna and flora were enriched. Migration after migration of animals came in from the mainland: deer, pigs, monkeys, orang-utans, elephants, rhinoceroses, tapirs, porcupines and a tremendous variety of birds and other creatures. New trees and other plants took hold in the Bornean forests. Sulawesi, by contrast, enjoyed no such contact with Asia and its forests have remained comparatively impoverished to this day. At the end of the last ice age the sea level rose

These jagged spires penetrating the forest canopy are all that remain of a large limestone hill. The limestone was eaten away over many millennia by acidic groundwater and heavy rains until the pinnacles were left standing free. Elsewhere in Borneo the action of water on limestone has created not spires, but great caves famous both for the wildlife they contain and for preserving relics of man's prehistory.

again, returning the three islands to their former isolation. But the rich influx from the mainland stayed on, free to develop and diversify.

The Bornean jungle is the climax of all these developments and its most striking feature is the bewildering variety of plants. Even an army of botanists would need many years to sort things out. There are thousands of species of tree alone, and they are jumbled together in the most haphazard confusion. Stands of a single species, a familiar sight in temperate woodlands, are unusual here. Over most of Borneo, a few acres may contain a varied collection of a hundred or more different species. Apart from the trees, there are many thousand other plant species to be accounted for in the rain forest. However, the jungle flora falls into some sort of order if you group plants by the way in which they obtain energy within the structure of the rain forest.

The upper storey of the forest is composed of the crowns of tall emergent trees, which take the lion's share of life-giving sunlight. A few species are sufficiently distinct to be immediately recognizable, such as the gnarled red belian, or ironwood, and the lofty mengaris trees whose feathery crowns emerge well above their neighbours, often over 250 feet from the ground. The majority of the large jungle trees, however, are hard to identify quickly. Among the most common are the dipterocarps, which have two-winged fruits, but there are several hundred species included in this family alone.

The chief difficulty for the botanist seeking to identify a tree is to get at the branches. Since the crowns of the trees mostly spread out a good hundred feet above the ground, leaving the interior of the forest almost dark, the only part of the tree easy to examine is the bare trunk. The texture of the bark, its colour when shaved with a knife, the smell and consistency of the sap may give useful clues. Even if you manage to get hold of a few leaves from the lofty canopy, they are not likely to be of much help, for most of the trees have remarkably similar leaves. What you really need to make a proper identification is a flower or fruit. There may be some flowers lying on the ground, but such finds are not conclusive evidence since it is impossible to be sure which of the trees produced them.

The scientific way to proceed is to get a flowering branch, complete with leaves. Once, it was fashionable to set half a dozen natives to work and fell one of the forest monsters, so that when it crashed to the ground, the botanist could pluck a blossom from the smashed crown and pop it into his vasculum for leisurely study later. Today it is usual to employ less wasteful methods. One famous botanist in Malaya even employed a monkey to collect tree-top flowers. Other common but less exotic methods include shooting down specimens with a rifle, and using specially trained Bornean tree climbers.

Even though the means of reaching the canopy exist, a flower may still be impossible to come by. Some trees, including the dipterocarps, flower only once every five to ten years. Many bloom irregularly, and may be triggered off by some change in the weather, such as a drought. The botanist, therefore, has to pounce whenever he happens to see an unidentified tree in flower and to keep a close watch over any particularly puzzling enigma, waiting for it to blossom—even though he may have to wait several years for this.

Shaded beneath the canopy are the plants of the middle storeys, a mixture of specialists adapted to living in the shade and slim saplings waiting for one of the giants to fall or a branch to snap—anything that will leave a hole in the canopy. For most saplings the opportunity never arises and they eventually die from lack of light. But occasionally sunshine will flood in through a gash in the top storey, and then the saplings grow at high speed. It is a race to the top. The first to get there will put out lateral branches, cutting off light from the rest. The losers are relegated to the shade.

There are, however, more ways for a plant to survive than by the haphazard method of struggling up through the dark layers below. Many plants live as epiphytes, anchoring themselves on branches and trunks. They have no connection with the ground, but collect their water and minerals from the damp nooks into which their roots grow. Dozens of species of orchids, mosses and ferns may festoon a single forest giant in addition to the climbing lianas and garlands of creepers that drape the branches and twine around the trunk.

One numerous group of Bornean plants, the strangling figs, are both tree-dwelling and ground-dwelling. The seedling fig starts life as an epiphyte in the crown of a large tree. Only after it has secured a place in the sun does it put out a thin descending root which eventually anchors in the soil of the forest floor and acts as a lifeline carrying water and mineral nutrients. As the fig grows, it sends down more and more of these descending roots, so many, in fact, that in the end it may smother the host tree, taking over not only the crown for its own branches and leaves, but also the dead trunk for support.

Down on the forest floor, the light is dim. Here there is no grass, little undergrowth, and only occasional plants living among the litter of fallen leaves: small palms, seedlings which are mostly short-lived, and damp-loving mosses. There are also two groups of plants, the parasites and saprophytes, which need no sunlight. Most noticeable are saprophytic fungi, which feed on decaying organic matter. In this world without clear seasons, trees shed their leaves all year round and the constant rain of debris from the upper layers provides a steady living for these scavengers of the plant world.

The parasites make up for the lack of sunlight by penetrating the tissues of other plants to steal nourishment. Borneo's most famous and spectacular parasitic plant is *Rafflesia*. It was discovered in 1818 and was named in honour of Sir Stamford Raffles, the founder of Singapore. He described the plant in confident Victorian terms as "the greatest prodigy of the vegetable world". It is an apt description.

Rafflesia gains its fame from its enormous flower, which is coloured in livid shades of red, white and brown; in Borneo it reaches sizes of over two feet across and weighs some 20 pounds. *Rafflesia* has no leaves, for it gets all its energy requirements from the tissues of a ground-trailing vine. It spends most of its life inside the host's stem as a network of threads, and becomes visible only when it flowers. After building up sufficient strength, a bud bursts out of the vine and gradually increases in size until it resembles a hard, brown cabbage. At last the five leathery petals open to reveal a central cup nearly a foot deep and studded with spikes. From the cup comes a powerful stench of something like rotting meat, and this attracts clouds of insects which act as pollinating agents. A search near the flower often reveals a couple of smaller buds awaiting their turn. Eventually a succession of giant blooms will open, all deriving their energy second-hand from the living cells of the vine.

Within the shady green habitat of the Bornean forest, the thousands of species of plants are linked in subtle ways with thousands of animal species to form an intricate web of life in which almost every conceivable niche has been exploited. Borneo is one of the places where nature has reached her greatest complexity of design, and this to me was one of the main attractions of the island. To see a strange plant or animal was to wonder what job it performed in the forest, and often the answers were to prove fascinating and exciting.

This wealth of living forms is, first of all, the result of Borneo's equatorial climate. Water and sunlight, the main requirements for plant growth, are constantly in plentiful supply. Two monsoons pour their rain over the island, one which blows up from the south and the other from the north-west. Between them the monsoons deliver at least 120

A rare parasite of woody vines, Rafflesia has one of the earth's largest flowers: each evil-smelling bloom spans more than two feet.

inches of rain a year. Temperatures remain high, with only slight fluctuations. The powerful sun shines on the canopy for five or six hours every day, and the air in the forest is always saturated with moisture. In these ideal surroundings most trees are permanently green.

With plants so productive, the food supply for animals is constant, never cut off by winter cold or long droughts. Every month provides its crop of flowers, fruit and new leaves, and animals can specialize in their feeding habits to an extent not possible in more seasonal habitats. Sunbirds can always find flowers, and gibbons and orang-utans are able to eat fruit all year round.

More important is the length of time over which these living forms have been able to develop. Time provides the chance for the divergent process of evolution to work, for new variations and adaptations to emerge, for new species and new genera to develop. This trend towards diversity is continually promoted by the interreactions between plants and animals. Many plants evolve hand in hand with insect pests and other herbivores which browse on their leaves, destroy their flowers or eat their seeds. To keep the animal pests off, the plants have evolved various defence mechanisms: some, for instance, are distasteful or poisonous; some maintain private armies of ants which live in their hollow stems. But if all used the same methods, they would be immediately vulnerable to any insect that broke the code. They get much better protection by diversifying, each species tending towards uniqueness.

Over millions of years, every advance by animal pests in seeking out plant hosts and breaking down their defences is countered by plants developing new defence mechanisms. Sometimes this process results in the emergence of a new species, which in turn leads to diversification of plant-eating animals: different species of insects and herbivores become specialized and build associations with particular plant species whose defences they are able to breach. Thus it is also an advantage to the plants to be widely scattered. They are more likely to escape detection by their pests if they grow apart rather than in a clump, since a solitary individual far from others of its own kind may well be missed. In all these ways evolution leads to the propagation of many rare species rather than domination by a few abundant ones.

The actual creation of such a diverse plant and animal community, however, takes millions of years of uninterrupted development. It may seem something of a riddle that Borneo, a young island, should display all the characteristics of a long biological history. But the explanation

Such is the multiplicity of plant adaptations in Borneo that some trees and vines, like those on the right, bear fruit directly on their trunks. Strings of edible yellow seeds hang from looping Gnetum vines, and bunches of fruit, like outsize grapes, festoon the trunks of Baccaurea trees. The fruits of the wild durian tree swell and burst on short stalks that spring from the bark, and edible varieties contain flesh so succulent that orang-utans seek them in spite of thorny spikes on the skins.

A GNETUM VINE

RIPENING DURIANS

A FRUITING BACCAUREA TREE

is simple. Much of its plant and animal community is older than the island itself. It consists largely of those species which had already shared a long history on the Asian mainland, evolving together as competitors for food and space, as predator and prey, host and parasite, before seeking refuge in tropical Sundaland during the ice ages. The largest surviving part of Sundaland is Borneo, and it is here that the greatest diversity of plants and animals has been preserved.

Only a large forest can support populations of rare and widely scattered species. In Borneo there are some trees so rare that they are known from only one or two specimens. Others may be so uncommon that only a few hundred individuals are scattered over the island. These trees quite possibly need thousands of square miles of forest to survive as a species. If the area available were to be reduced, their total numbers might fall to a level where sufficient genetic exchange between individuals could no longer take place. The species would fail to maintain itself and finally cease to exist; any animal dependents would die out too.

The forests of Borneo are shrinking every year. The high price of timber and the arrival of mechanized logging are causing destruction at a frightening pace. Within the next few decades almost all the accessible areas of jungle may well have been felled by the timber companies. Secondary forest will grow quickly, but it may take several hundreds of years for a forest community like the original to be restored. Felling will probably occur again before that happens. Consequently the variety of Bornean wildlife is threatened. Setting aside representative blocks of forest as national parks or nature reserves will provide refuges from which many species may be able to recolonize the devastated forest areas, but they probably will not be large enough to ensure the survival of all the rare plants and animals.

The rarest plants are likely to vanish first as their numbers reach the threshold of population collapse, and with them will go their specific parasites. Gradually the whole pyramid of ecological relationships will be eroded. The wide-ranging animals—elephants, rhinoceroses, orangutans, and big predators like the clouded leopard—will lose their habitats and disappear. Something lush and tropical will remain, but Borneo's claim to be one of the richest corners of the earth for plant and animal life may well be lost for ever.

Not until recently did man have so severe an effect on the Bornean jungle. For many millennia he lived on more equal terms with nature, and his occupation probably began as long ago as the ice ages. Like other animals on the Asian mainland, early man found that the tropical climate of the newly exposed Sundaland shelf made an attractive refuge, and he joined the great migrations. *Homo erectus* is known to have reached Java, and he probably arrived in Borneo as well. However, he left no traces of his presence, and archaeology records only the presence of modern man, *Homo sapiens*. An unbroken succession of human remains can be traced back 50,000 years in the Great Cave at Niah, on the northwest coast of Borneo.

From the earliest times, human influence in Borneo has been concentrated around the coasts and along the major waterways. The rounded shape of the island means that the interior is much larger and more difficult to penetrate than, say, a long thin island like Java or a deeply embayed one like Sulawesi. Only small populations lived inland among the rolling tracts of unknown jungle between the rivers, and their reduced numbers made little impact on the forest.

These people were usually the remnants of coastal dwellers who had been displaced and forced back by wave after wave of later invaders and immigrants arriving by raft and canoe. Negritos were pushed back by Australoid races. The Australoids in their turn were conquered by the Mongoloid proto-Malays, head-hunters who swept into Borneo in three violent waves: first the Kenyah, then the Kayans, and finally the warrior Ibans, the most blood-thirsty of all the invaders.

Apart from the Negritos, elements of all these tribes survive today and are commonly grouped under the blanket title of Dyaks, the famous Wild Men of Borneo. Among the Australoid peoples, nomadic Punans wander over the Usun Apau plateau and other remote areas. Kelabits still erect megalithic burial monuments in the highlands further north. Muruts and Dusuns occupy the north-eastern corner of the island, while the Njadjus are found in the south. The last conquerors, the Ibans, are the most numerous. During my time in Borneo I was to come into contact with several of the Dyak peoples, especially the Dusuns and Ibans. I found that although they differ greatly in origins and beliefs, they all bear a recognizably Bornean stamp, something intrinsic to the rugged mountains, lush jungle and swirling rivers that have forced a wild way of life upon them.

Trading peoples settled around the coasts of Borneo in much the same way as the indigenous tribesmen. Before the last two centuries their numbers and influence remained very small, but there have been Chinese trading posts on the north and west coasts of Borneo for over 1,000 years, from the time of the T'ang dynasty. From here a wealth of goods was exported to mainland China: gold, minerals, edible birds' nests, rhinoceros horn, colourful feathers, hornbill ivory, beeswax, camphor, sandalwood, and other riches of the forest. These wares were paid for in coins, glass beads, and large pots which are still treasured in the *kampong*, or villages, of the interior. The Dyaks call them dragon jars, after the serpents winding around the outsides under the brown glaze.

Other traders visited Borneo, including the Malays who established a large sultanate centred on Brunei in the 15th Century. Europeans did not arrive until the 16th Century, and for a long time they, too, made very little impact on the forest in their search for the island's natural wealth. It was not until 1521 that the first fully recorded visit was made to Borneo. Magellan's fleet was voyaging in search of the Spice Islands, an undertaking that was eventually to take it right round the world. After visiting the Philippines, where Magellan was killed, the ships put into the harbour of Brunei. Pigafetta, the expedition's chronicler, left a glowing account of the splendours of the town, including the stilted houses which must have looked much as they do today. Magellan's crew were greatly impressed by the abundance of gold, porcelain and silk in the sultan's palace, and it was from a corruption of the name Brunei that the whole island became known to Europeans.

During the next four centuries, the European nations began accumulating empires, eventually claiming as their own every part of the world that they came across. But they had little success with Borneo. Apart from being difficult to control on account of its vast interior, the island has few natural harbours. The British and the Dutch tried to establish trading stations, but time after time had to admit defeat.

It was only in the 19th Century that Europeans finally managed to establish a foothold in Borneo and to penetrate its forests. In 1839, a young British adventurer, James Brooke, was visiting Brunei in his armed sailing ship when the sultan asked for his aid in dealing with rebels in one of his outlying provinces. He even offered to make Brooke a rajah and gave him Sarawak to rule if he would stay and help. At first Brooke refused this extraordinary offer, but in the end he accepted. The rebels were put down, and they surrendered on condition that Brooke did indeed become their rajah. So was established the romantic dynasty of the White Rajahs who ruled Sarawak in a fashion both benevolent and autocratic for more than a hundred years.

Borneo had been drawn into the orbit of the modern world. In the colonial period of the island's history, the British took control of the north, establishing a protectorate over Brunei and a chartered company

A sunlit sweep of river creates a wide gap in the tree cover of the lowland swamp forest. Thousands of different species of trees flourish in Borneo's warm, even climate. They form so dense a canopy that little sunlight reaches the ground, except where an old tree has fallen or where rivers like this one cut their erratic paths through the swampy areas.

(later a colony) in North Borneo, and the Dutch took over eastern and southern parts of Borneo. For the first time, the great forest of the interior was explored, and the scientific documentation of its plants and animals began. Much of the early research was done by colonial officials who took a keen interest in botany or zoology. The first Rajah Brooke made his own collections as well as patronizing other scientific research. His secretary, Spenser St. John, who later became British Consul-General in Brunei, was another accomplished naturalist.

St. John got to know Hugh Low, the Colonial Secretary on the island of Labuan. The two men often travelled together in Borneo and made a joint exploration of Mount Kinabalu. Some important collecting took place on their trips, and St. John showed a flair for the description and understanding of plants which seems not to have been uncommon in the colonial administration of those days. He recorded how on one occasion "Mr. Low found a beautiful gardinia, growing on slight elevations, on barren, decomposing rock, and plentiful wherever the land was undulating. It seemed to flourish in positions exposed to the hottest rays of the sun, and in situations where the reflected heat was also very great. It was a bush, varying from a few inches to two feet in height, and bore flowers of a pure white. We observed some of the shrubs not six inches in height, which were covered with blossoms, yielding a powerful aromatic odour. In fact as we rode among them, the whole air appeared filled with their fragrance. I imagine the dwarfing of the plants resulted from the inferior nature of the soil and the great heat which kept the moisture from their roots." Such an accurate ecological description would be the envy of many a modern botanist.

The first trained naturalist to work in Borneo was the Dutch botanist, Pieter Willem Korthals, who arrived in 1836. Other scientists followed in his wake: Odoardo Beccari, a distinguished Italian botanist who reached the island in 1865, and John Whitehead, a British ornithologist whose magnificently illustrated book on The Exploration of Mount Kina Balu recorded the first intensive survey of the mountain's varied flora and fauna. Among the most recent professionals to work in Borneo was Tom Harrisson, curator of the famous Sarawak Museum. During his time, while dealing in great detail and depth with the zoology, ornithology, ethnography and archaeology of his huge parish, he and his wife, Barbara, started the series of historic excavations in the Great Cave at Niah, which have provided so much information about the island's past.

Among the explorer naturalists of the 19th Century, one name stands out above all others. Alfred Russel Wallace was a professional zoological collector, gathering specimens to sell to the wealthy amateur scientists of Victorian England. When he arrived in Sarawak in 1855, Rajah Brooke offered him hospitality. The two men, it appears, got on very well together and debated questions of science and theology late into the night. The Rajah lent Wallace his country house on the coast at Santubong. There Wallace worked on his collections and wrote a paper entitled *On the Law Which Has Regulated the Introduction of New Species.* In it, he pointed out that species were not nearly so distinct from each other as naturalists had supposed and that often forms differed from each other only by a few seemingly trivial characteristics. Species, he argued, had arisen not from separate acts of divine creation as postulated by many theologians, but by natural variability. He illustrated his points with butterflies, beetles and weevils which he had gathered in the Bornean forest. That paper was arguably the most important contribution to evolutionary theory before the publication of Darwin's work. It led Wallace to write a further paper proposing a theory that was identical to the one Darwin himself had developed a few years earlier but had not yet published. Eventually both papers were read together at the historic meeting of the Linnean Society in London in 1858, which publicly proclaimed for the first time the theory of evolution by natural selection.

The Bornean forest, therefore, can properly be credited with having stimulated one of the most important theories in zoology and, some might say, in the philosophy of science. It is an impressive claim to fame, but there is a great deal more to be learned yet from Borneo. In spite of the tremendous efforts of those researchers who have worked there, the island remains far from fully explored. By 1950 only 85,000 botanical specimens had been collected, the equivalent of just one specimen for every 2,000 acres of jungle.

We are a long way from fully understanding the whole forest ecosystem—indeed every discovery highlights new areas of our ignorance —but we must try to learn all we can while these magnificent forests remain. It was with a great feeling of enthusiasm, but also of responsibility, that I set out into the Bornean jungle to start my own exploration.

Plants that Grow without Sunlight

On the gloomy floor of the Bornean jungle, among the fallen leaves and rotting logs, there sprouts a dazzling array of tropical fungi. These decay-promoting plants grow in an inexplicable profusion of colours and shapes. Some even glow in the dark, and the maiden's veil garbs its stem with a fine crinoline net worthy of the purest bride.

No one can fully explain what benefit the Bornean fungi derive from such extravagant permutations. Perhaps some of the colours serve to warn fungus-eating animals that the tissues have poisonous properties. Or these plants simply may have diversified in a reckless response to the ideal growing conditions: high humidity, warm temperature and the constant rain of organic matter from the canopy above.

This decaying vegetation provides most fungi with all the nutrients they need, for they do not rely on sunlight as a source of energy and can live in the darkest places. The main body of each fungus, the mycelium, usually lives out of sight below the ground, spreading out in a network of fine, hair-like filaments which permeate rotting matter, breaking it down into digestible form.

As the mycelium matures, it develops small nodules that grow upwards and finally emerge into the open air. These become the fruiting bodies, commonly known as mushrooms and toadstools. Although they may survive for only a few days or, in some cases, a few hours, the fruiting bodies are vital to the perpetuation of their species, for they produce thousands of spores which will grow into new fungi.

The instantly recognizable mushroom types produce the spores beneath their fleshy caps and liberate them, when ripe, to be wafted away by gentle air currents. Other fungi, which also rely on air currents for dispersal, produce their spores high up on tentacle-like branches. The fairy clubs are one such group, and their fruiting bodies stick up from the forest floor like miniature trees in winter or like pieces of coral.

The maiden's veil has a quite different dispersal mechanism, and few Bornean travellers forget it. During its mature life of less than a day, the fungus gives off a most unmaidenly smell, sickly and penetrating. This attracts insects to come and feed on the sticky, spore-laden cap crowning its stem. When the insects leave, the spores stick to them and are carried away.

Glowing in the dead of night, the gills of a Mycena cyanophos fungus emit enough light for it to be photographed without a flash. This luminous quality seems to be the result of certain enzymes combining with oxygen, but its purpose is unknown. The light may warn nocturnal beetles not to eat this species.

In brief resplendence, a maiden's veil has attracted a red beetle by its strong smell, but soon the odour will fade and the fine net wilt.

Looking more like leafless trees than fungi, these fruiting bodies of a fairy club species produce countless spores along their branches.

A *Cookeiana tricholoma* holds its spores inside a cup lined with hairs.

The brilliance of these fairy clubs remains unexplained. Perhaps the scarlet colour is a chance result of their chemical structure.

In a fleshy whorl, Stereum ostrea sprouts from a fallen forest tree.

A prolific cluster of toadstools in various stages of development indicates that there is a large body of fungal growth beneath the ground.

2/ Life in the Great Forest

If you step out of the radius of your camp-fires you feel that you are brought face to face with forces over which you have no sort of control; you are surrounded on all sides by handiwork that is not man's, by swarming millions of creatures that live out their little lives without the faintest reference to you. ROBERT W. C. SHELFORD/ *A NATURALIST IN BORNEO*

If you really want to see the Bornean jungle you must journey to the headwaters of one of the major rivers, away from the villages and towns of the coast. Once your dugout canoe has passed the last long-house or *kampong*, the scenery and atmosphere change. You enter a world essentially unchanged during the millions of years of man's evolution.

My own initiation took place in Sabah. I travelled by *sampan* up the Segama river, which drains the mountains of the Brassey range before winding eastwards to the warm waters of the Sulu Sea. The Segama is a moody, powerful river, sometimes meandering deep and slow, sometimes rushing over curving sandbanks where the water is so shallow that the boat must be hauled. Where it has carved a narrow gorge through the hard bedrock, the river boils and spumes as the swirling waters race through the constriction, pouring down violent rapids into the frothing pool below. My Iban companions were born and bred to such hazards and our *sampan* made good headway against the tugging currents. Ibans are the traditional Wild Men of Borneo, but these were good guardians to me. It was a strange thought, though, that as recently as the Second World War they were still head-hunting, turning their bloodthirsty warrior cult against the Japanese occupation forces.

White cave-pocked cliffs gave way to the monotony of towering green forest on either bank. Hour after hour we wound our tortuous way beneath the blazing sun. There are still crocodiles in the Segama in spite of much over-hunting, but the only large reptile we saw was a monitor lizard, a six-foot monster basking on a rock. At our approach he raised his long slender head and scuttled into the water. Here and there we spotted brilliant kingfishers, troops of chattering monkeys, and the occasional hornbills, enormous dark birds with outsize, down-curving bills. For me it was a frustrating journey. I longed to have more than these tantalizing glimpses, to call a halt, pull the boat into the bank and set foot inside the enveloping shade of the forest. But this was sheer impatience. I would soon have ample time to explore, for it would be three months before I was to return downriver.

At nightfall we camped on a small island. After the long and exhausting day, we slept oblivious to the chorus of night creatures and the gurgle of the river. Next morning the Ibans dropped me on a sandy beach at the point where the main river is joined by its tributary, the Bole river. It was here that I was to rendezvous with two Dusuns I had engaged to bring up my supplies.

Right now I was alone. The Dusuns with their heavily-laden boat would not catch up for at least another two days. Slightly apprehensive, I set out on a preliminary excursion into the dense, green and secretive forest. I was immediately struck by its magnificence. Giant trees towered up 150 feet or more from vast buttress roots, their crowns hidden from view by the thick canopy of lower trees. Little light penetrated to the ground, so vegetation cover was sparse and walking quite easy. There were hazards though—sharp *Pandanus* leaves, barbed rattan tendrils and multitudes of revolting leeches that looped towards me wherever I went. These were far too plentiful to burn off or douse with salt as the textbooks advise, so I pulled them free and hoped that the bleeding wounds would not become infected.

I found the terrain surprisingly hilly and after a couple of hours I was tired and soaked with perspiration. My legs were sore and bleeding from scratches and the leech bites. So great was the exertion of travel that I had little chance to look for signs of animal life. In fact the forest seemed to be deserted. I set a compass course back to the Segama and was heartily relieved when I finally emerged at a point overlooking the beach where I had been dropped by my Iban companions. I bathed my hot and weary body in the cool, muddy water, ate a tin of meat and made myself a rough bed under a canvas sheet.

Over the next two days I got to know more about my surroundings and familiarized myself with the nearby streams and ridges. I began to hear and see some of the forest creatures that had eluded me at first: chirping birds, wild pigs and monkeys. When I discovered footprints of the two-horned rhinoceros, one of Borneo's rarest animals, and followed this up by meeting a family of red-haired orang-utans, I was really excited about my new environment. When my two Dusuns eventually arrived with the rest of my food and equipment, I decided we need travel no farther up-river and instructed them to cut wood for a *pondok*, or open-walled shelter, and set up camp on the riverbank.

We quickly established a routine. The Dusuns fished in the river and looked after the camp, providing me with a permanent base, while I made daily sorties into the forest to study its wildlife. As I discovered better paths and learned to recognise my surroundings, I began to feel more at home. Even the leeches became less of a horror.

There were two common species of leech. One rather drab, brown fellow remained on the ground and usually climbed straight down inside my shoes to feed around my ankles. The other was bigger and more colourful—orange, striped with yellow and black. Firmly attached to a leaf, up to two feet above ground, it would wave its trunk-like body, ready to adhere to any creature that brushed by. It also had a rather uncanny ability to leap. If it could sense me standing just out of reach, it hung limply, raised its anterior slightly, then swung forwards, simultaneously releasing its posterior sucker. Thus it could jump ahead a few inches, either landing with a slap on my leg or falling short on to the forest floor. If it missed its target it would loop remorselessly across the ground in pursuit of me.

Leeches are equipped with three circular teeth inside the anterior sucker. Having found a suitable attachment on my body, each loathsome creature would cut a Y-shaped hole, pump anti-coagulant into the wound and feast on my blood. The whole process was so well lubricated that unless a nerve was cut I did not feel a thing. Often it was only after the bloated leech had released its hold and fallen to the ground that I spotted the tell-tale blood from the oozing wound.

Ticks, biting flies, heat and humidity, and tropical downpours all added to the hardship of life, but gradually I grew accustomed to these discomforts and discovered that the forest was actually a very peaceful and rewarding place. When I became in tune, so to speak, I found that all around there was constant noise: buzzing cicadas and crickets, burping lizards and frogs, and a chorus of bird and monkey calls. The mood varied according to the time of day, but always the sounds had a lulling, almost hypnotic, effect on me.

In spite of all this evidence of active life, it took me a long time to see

Three inches of slimy flatworm slide across a wet leaf on the forest floor. Flatworms are traditionally aquatic organisms, but inside the forest the ground is so damp that some types like this are able to lead a completely terrestrial existence. If the primitive flatworms are starved of the microscopic animals they eat, many absorb their own vital systems in order of importance, starting with the reproductive organs and ending with the nerves.

more than a fraction of what I heard. I could walk for hours through the green naves of the forest without seeing a single large animal. I knew animals were there, and in great variety—not only pigs and rhinos, but deer, wild cattle, bears and even elephants—but they were shy and uncommon in comparison with the abundant big game that roams the tropical savannahs. Open country, where grass and shrubs flourish, can support herds of ungulates and, preying upon them, numerous carnivores. Here, by contrast, where ground herbage was so sparse, there were few big herbivores—and consequently few big carnivores.

The popular idea of the jungle as a dangerous place full of ferocious animals is, therefore, quite unrealistic. There are no tigers or panthers in Borneo, and the largest predator is the beautiful clouded leopard which is notoriously shy of man. Although sun bears are common and nearly every tree is scarred with their claw marks, these small black marauders are normally afraid of man and keep well out of his way.

This is not to say that anyone who spends a long time in the forest will never get a scare. I once had a nasty experience with two sun bears. They have very poor eyesight, and a mother and her cub blundered dangerously close before they saw me. Instead of fleeing, they rushed, roaring bad temperedly, towards me. Their sharp, slashing feet and powerful jaws can do a lot of damage, and I escaped unharmed only by fighting them off with my *parang* and injuring the cub. While the mother went to its aid, I hastily made my getaway.

But such frightening incidents were rare. On subsequent encounters with sun bears I cut a sapling and waved it vigorously about, shouting to warn them of my presence before they came too close. Invariably they hurried away. Nor was I ever troubled by snakes. Twenty-foot pythons can tackle wild pig and deer, but they would not attack a fully grown man. There were poisonous cobras, kraits and pit vipers, but on the rare times I saw them, they hurried out of my way. In fact, for some strange reason, the incidence of snake bite in Borneo is much lower than in other tropical regions. All in all the Bornean forest seemed a pretty safe place to be, and I never had any qualms about wandering there alone. The threat from animals was far less than the danger of getting lost or being hit by a falling tree. Indeed the risks of motoring that we accept so readily on our modern roads and highways are probably far greater than those taken by the jungle traveller.

It was pleasant to have a camp with the comforts of a fire and cheerful company to return to each night after my wanderings in the forest, but sometimes it proved inconvenient to head back for home in the evening.

If only I could sleep out under the trees, I thought, I would be able to range much farther from the river. Also, if I found interesting animals to watch, I would be able to continue my observations right up to nightfall and resume them again at dawn.

Accordingly, now that I felt quite at ease in the forest by day, I decided to expand my experience. I spent my first anxious night away from camp curled beneath the protective buttresses of a great tree with a plastic cape for shelter. I did not sleep very long. Before I could detect the faintest glimmer of daylight, I was awake, cold and stiff but still intact. Perhaps it was the discomfort that had disturbed me, or it may have been the subtle change in the forest sounds. The first insects and birds were already calling tentatively and soon I heard a solitary male gibbon start to give voice before his neighbours. I had eaten a quick snack and packed my simple sleeping quarters before the first slanting grey rays of dawn broke through the cold mist of the forest morning.

Confident that I need no longer be tied to camp, I embarked on more ambitious trips into the forest. Sometimes I went off for several days at a time, and over the next few weeks I did have one or two disturbed nights. Once a porcupine wanted to pass where I was lying and refused to make a detour around me. Not wanting to argue the matter, I moved and let it trundle through on what was obviously its habitual path.

Several times I heard elephants crashing around nearby and I then became rather uneasy. Elephants are unpredictable creatures. Sometimes they flee at the first sniff of man, sometimes they pay no attention. But one night I had to move my sleeping quarters several times in an attempt to throw off a huge beast that seemed to be pursuing me. Eventually I found sanctuary among the buttress roots of one of the forest giants. On two other occasions I had to scurry up trees to get out of the paths of some angry, charging bulls.

Nevertheless, I began quite to enjoy my solitary existence in the forest. Above all it gave me a unique opportunity to learn about the animals that are seen only at night, and I always looked forward to the thrilling moment when the forest communities changed shifts. The transition from jungle day to jungle night is sudden and dramatic. As dusk falls, the bush crickets strike up their mechanical wailing, and tree-frogs begin their chorus. Nightjars circle overhead, mewing plaintively. The mantle of blackness rapidly envelops the forest floor and spreads up through the canopy. Then at the key moment, the bush crickets grow quiet and ground crickets emerge from their burrows and launch into a

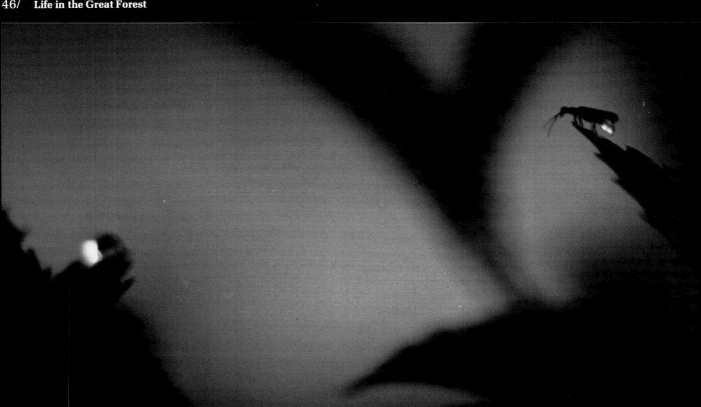

As the sun goes down, two adult male fireflies send out signals, each in time with the other, in a joint effort to attract mates.

Shining steadily from its tail, a glow-worm warns predators that it is distasteful.

The Luminous Beetles

Early most nights, the Bornean forests are lit by the tiny lamps of certain beetles and their larvae. Known as fireflies if they have wings and glow-worms if they do not, these insects produce their cold light from glands that secrete a luminous compound.

Glow-worms (*left*) cast a continuous light as a warning mechanism; adult male fireflies, on the other hand, flash at regular intervals to attract mates. *Pteropteryx malaccae* males, which are found in mangrove trees, light up once every three-quarters of a second. Often they join forces in an irresistible synchronous display (*right*), thousands flashing together in perfect unison. Mating occurs as the attracted females rush along the lighted branches, finding partners simply by colliding with them.

In this time-exposure in which stars appear like comets, a whole tree glitters with male fireflies maximizing their attractive potential.

pulsating, monotonous buzz. The change-over is complete. The creatures of the day have retired to their nests and sleeping posts, and the nocturnal community has taken over.

The darkness seems total. Even the faint light of the sky and stars is blotted out by the thick blanket of vegetation. But there is some light of another sort, very faint like a phosphorescent mist. The forest floor is studded with tiny luminous spots and veins where the bacteria and delicate fungal filaments on the rotting leaf litter glow with a living light. Clumps of fragile toadstools shine ghostly green. Glow-worms sparkle in the leaf litter and shrub layer: long, thin ones, small flat ones; I saw one peculiar maggot-like form with eight yellow gleaming spots on each side. Flying fireflies add their display to the illuminations, flashing out messages of species and sex as they sail through the canopy.

Now that it is dark, the earthworms start work. They are vital to the nutrient cycle of the forest—for their activity in breaking down rotting leaves. Each worm seizes a dead leaf and drags it into the sanctuary of its burrow where it digests everything of value. The remains of the leaf are excreted as liquid earth to form a cast. Since the ground is so humid the earthworm must build the cast up into a vertical trumpet so that the semi-viscous waste will not slide back into the burrows. As the cast hardens it projects like a minaret above the ground.

These earthworms provide feasts for the moonrat, a nocturnal creature and a relation of shrews and hedgehogs, although it looks like a large rat with a furry white coat. It has a thick, naked tail and its long, sensitive snout is decorated with a ridiculous pink rosette at the tip. The moonrat is so foul-smelling and distasteful to predators that it requires no camouflage, and its startling white coat clearly advertises its unpleasant identity. It is so conspicuous against the backdrop of dark forest that not even those night hunters with a poor sense of smell, like the owls, are unlikely to mistake the moonrat for a juicy titbit.

I frequently met these strange animals on my night forays. They made no attempt to run away but shuffled on unhurriedly. If they felt threatened, however, the moonrats performed a frightening display. They turned on me, snarling ferociously with mouths open, exhibiting dangerous rows of jagged teeth. This aggressive demonstration must surely be an adequate defence against any would-be predator that had not already read the warning signs.

An equally effective defence mechanism belongs to another of the nocturnal animals, the pangolin, or scaly anteater. Pangolins look like miniature dinosaurs in suits of armour, for they are covered with over-lapping scaly plates with a sheen like burnished medieval steel. When they feel endangered, they roll up into a ball, wrapping their strong armoured tails over their heads for double protection, and so present an exterior that few predators can tackle.

Pangolins are rather particular about their food and prefer to stick to a rich diet of ant eggs and grubs. A sharp-clawed pangolin can quickly rip open an ant nest or termite mound and probe the galleries inside with its long sticky tongue, taking quick mouthfuls of the grubs which adhere to the tongue's surface. Often, however, the pangolin fails to finish off the coveted prize, for when the irate ants swarm out to attack, it goes quickly on the retreat.

One day in camp a visiting tribesman brought me a female pangolin with a small baby riding on her tail and I thought I would get a chance to observe the creature's habits more closely. The mother was rather shy but the baby lapped up tinned milk from a cup. I put them both in a rattan basket to prevent them escaping in the night, but I had greatly under-estimated the pangolin's strength. In the morning the basket was empty and a ragged hole showed where the scaly creatures had forced their exit. (The Dusuns had a particularly apt description for that gaping basket: they said it was *ketawa*, or laughing.)

I did have plenty of chances to observe another common nocturnal creature. Wherever I slept out in the forest, I was visited by a tangalung, which is a big, rather primitive, omnivorous civet with a blotched coat, barred tail, and vivid black and white stripes on the side of the neck. This was a bold creature who licked clean any cans I had lying around and sometimes came sniffing right up to my face. Even when I shone my torch at him he remained quite unafraid, his dark eyes reflecting the light with steely gaze. Since I slept at different sites, often a considerable distance apart, but was always visited by this same civet, he must have had a very large territory as well as a good sense of smell to find me.

Usually the tangalung feeds on centipedes which can grow up to seven inches long and are armed with powerful pincer jaws and poison glands. I had the misfortune to be visited by one of these, too. One night as I lay in camp, I was suddenly awakened by a sharp, stabbing pain on my forehead. I grabbed for a torch and mirror and to my horror saw two small, bleeding punctures in the fast inflaming weal. I was just resigning myself to a painful death from snakebite when I heard something scuttling across the floor of the hut. The torch beam revealed the culprit, a huge centipede making its getaway. I chopped the creature in half with my *parang*, swallowed a couple of antihistamine tablets to reduce any allergic reaction, and returned to my couch, much relieved that my attacker had not been a snake.

Some nights when I could not sleep, I explored the forest by torchlight, and it was on such occasions that I came across the delicate mouse deer, tiny creatures barely 12 inches high. Mouse deer are very timid and I rarely saw them by day, but at night they were dazzled by the light of my torch and I could come within a few feet of them. Their large eyes would shine brightly in the glare as they sat beneath a swarm of mosquitoes or moved unhurriedly over the forest floor, boldly sampling fallen fruit close in front of me. The mouse deer is not a true deer but a survival from a primitive family, the Tragulidae, which was widespread in Asia 12 million years ago. It certainly looks like a deer, in spite of its size, but the males bear no antlers and, unlike the true deer, both sexes have long, sharp, canine teeth.

During the daytime the only terrestrial animals I saw regularly were roaming wild pigs which dashed off in single file at my approach, snorting their disapproval. Nevertheless, the forest floor teemed with smaller life, especially insects of all kinds, and on my travels I found plenty to interest me. I was particularly struck by the ants that swarmed everywhere in a constant frenzy of activity—over the ground, on low-growing vegetation, and even inside plants. Very conspicuous were the giant ants, an inch and a half long, marching along singly or in small parties. These ants have strong jaws, and can squirt a powerful acid from their rears. If provoked they can inflict terrible damage, but normally they are not aggressive and although I often found them marching all over me, I was never bitten. The same cannot be said of the ferocious ponerine ants, however, which will give a painful sting to anyone who gets in their way. These shiny black insects belong to a primitive ant group with a very crude social organization and live under logs where they search in hunting parties for millepedes. Having found a victim, they drag it back alive to their nest and cut it up to feed their grubs.

I frequently saw armies of tree ants, *Crematogaster*, crawling over paths and rotten logs, flowing endlessly up thick trunks, marching in long unbroken lines as they carried food to their nests. These moving columns were rather like conveyor belts. As each worker arrived at the nest, it deposited its burden, then turned back to search for more, and rejoined the end of the column so that the line was never interrupted. The tree ants were conspicuous with tiny triangular yellow or black abdomens. Normally they carried these triangles steadily aloft but if

A mouse deer, one of the smallest of all hoofed animals, picks a timid path through the thick undergrowth in which it spends the day.

disturbed, they rushed about waggling them madly, and so passing the danger signal quickly along the column. Given the opportunity, they could inflict a vicious bite.

One of the most fascinating things about the tree ants is that they enjoy mutualistic relationships with a variety of Bornean plants. I first came across this phenomenon when I unwittingly knocked against a thick, spiny rattan cane that looped across my path. To my surprise the whole cane began to echo with a rhythmic, synchronous rustling, which continued for half a minute before gradually dying down. I knocked the cane again and the rattling started once more. On closer examination I could see that where the leaves grew out from the stem of the cane they were swollen to form hollow shelters. Inside were many ants, and it was their rhythmic movements against the dry, ridged leaf sheath that produced the strange rustling. Small holes at the base of the sheaths provided the ants with an entrance and exit.

The ants were not damaging any living tissue of the plant and the structural design of the rattan seemed positively to encourage lodgers. Perhaps the presence of ants is in the plant's interest. They may well provide an additional defence mechanism against those animals which, undaunted by the spiny coat, attempt to eat the cane. The rattling message certainly seemed to warn "keep off". Elephants feed extensively on canes and they may well be deterred by the knowledge that this particular one is alive with biting ants.

That a plant should adapt its leaves for ant habitation seemed surprising enough, but I was fascinated by the lengths to which other plants had gone in providing ant hostels right inside their stems, and I spent a long time examining these Bornean specialities. The shrub *Macaranga caladifolia*, for example, has hollow stems perforated by small holes and it seems so anxious to harbour ants that it produces a special food to draw them to it. The basal leaf veins terminate in glands that exude sweet fluids attractive to ants. The *Macaranga* clearly benefits from its guests, for severe caterpillar damage occurs on those shrubs that are without resident ants. This valuable protective service to plants was recognized centuries ago by Chinese farmers who suspended bamboo bridges between bushes in orange groves to enable the ants to move freely among them.

Many of the ant plants are epiphytic, and I particularly noticed a small bushy shrub, *Hydnophytum*, which had a roughly spherical swelling at the base of its stem. This tuber was often as large as a man's head and had many large holes leading to the ant galleries within. Another ant-harbouring type, *Myrmecodia tuberosa*, a member of the bedstraw family, had a ridged bottle-like swelling on the base of its single stem; this, too, was riddled with tunnels.

Epiphytes benefit rather differently from ant occupation for it is not so much protection that they get but minerals which they cannot obtain in the normal way because they have no connection with the ground. The ants, in return for shelter, provide the host with their mineral-rich excreta. When I sliced open a *Myrmecodia* tuber I found that some of the galleries were occupied by ants while others were being used as disposal units and were packed with earth and ant debris. To exploit this supply, the *Myrmecodia* actually had fine roots growing into its own galleries.

No one who has spent any amount of time in the Bornean rain forest can fail to notice a multiplicity of other insects and their subtle variations of colour and form. Some are brightly coloured, others merge into their background. Some look like flowers and others possess ingenious mechanisms to frighten off predators. In their many adaptations, the Bornean insects have exploited to the full the opportunities for obtaining food and avoiding the multitude of mammals, birds, lizards and toads—not to mention other insects—ready to devour them.

The most conspicuous and brightly coloured insects are usually unattractive to predators. They may be hard and spiny, fierce-jawed or stinging, or they may produce foul-tasting, evil-smelling fluids. By advertising their unpleasantness with bright colours they give a warning to predators to keep away.

Just as easily, however, a quite palatable species might "cheat" and adopt the appearance of some distasteful type, to its obvious advantage. On my walks in the forest I became fascinated by the number of insects that mimicked the mutillid wasps in this fashion. There were several species of these wasps in Borneo, all displaying the same striking red, black and white warning colours. I often saw the gaudy wingless females scurrying jerkily among the leaf litter, the black abdomen splashed with white and the head and thorax bright red. But sometimes I found I was mistaken and had discovered instead a cricket, roach or spider, perfect in its mimicry of both the colour and gait of the stinging model. Most ingenious of all was the little coreid bug. It accurately copied the colours of the mutillid wasp, but in reverse, having its head and thorax black with white markings and its abdomen bright red. The reason for this reversal seems to lie in the strange sex life of the bug. Coreids spend most of their adult life joined tail to tail with their mating partners.

An Asiatic horned toad scours the forest floor for insects and slugs, protected from predators by its elaborate camouflage. The toad's angular lines and the horn-like flaps of skin on the head, from which its name derives, combine with its colour to create an almost perfect simulation of the surrounding litter of dead leaves.

These duos walk freely about the forest floor in tandem, the leader travelling head first and the other walking backwards. Thus whichever one leads, the last portion will be black and white, like the abdomen of the mutillid wasp, even though it is in fact a head.

Those insects which are neither distasteful nor look unpalatable have other ways of avoiding predators. Some hide in holes and emerge only at night, or shelter behind their own cryptic camouflage, disguised as leaves or twigs. Others combine camouflage with "startle" mechanisms, bright markings which are suddenly exposed to surprise an attacking bird and give the insect time to escape.

Camouflage is not merely the art of being hidden from predators, however; predators themselves may be disguised so that their prey will approach within striking distance. Perhaps the most exotic example of a predator adopting camouflage is the flower mantis. The mantis nymph resembles a flower, often an orchid, and the limbs have papery, petaloid extensions which simulate not only the shape and colour of petals but even their semi-opalescent texture. I found two white mantises in the forest; but pink and yellow specimens have also been collected, for this creature can change its colour to suit its surroundings. In fact, merely by placing one of my white mantises in a jar with a pink paper disc, I was able to induce a noticeable colour change in a couple of days, even though the insect did not moult. When I placed the other one on some flowers, it looked just like a blossom and I watched it trick and devour a quick succession of bees and flies until its normally flat, petal-like abdomen was swollen tight.

One of the major difficulties of studying wildlife in Borneo is that the richest diversity of species is found in the tree canopy, more than 100 feet above ground. It is here that most of the sunlight is trapped by green leaves and converted through photosynthesis into the primary plant foods that support herbivores and, in turn, carnivores. To observe these animals you need good hearing, a pair of binoculars and a good deal of experience in knowing what to look for. Consequently the life of the canopy was one of the last aspects of the forest that I came to terms with, but it was one of the most rewarding and I spent much of my time in Borneo lying on my back.

In spite of the good food supply, life in the canopy has its problems. During the day it is much hotter and drier up there than on the dim forest floor. Drinking water is available only in a few tree holes. Most important, of course, the wide gaps between adjacent crowns and the varying size and load-bearing capacity of the intermeshing branches make movement difficult.

Birds and bats have a natural advantage over other forms of canopy life. Yet a surprising number of wingless mammals, reptiles and even amphibians also live in the treetops: ranging from monkeys and squirrels, to lizards, snakes and frogs. Although these climbing creatures are somewhat at a disadvantage when travelling, they capitalize on other specialities. Squirrels with their rodent teeth feed on a variety of hard fruits and woody materials that bats and birds are not able to tackle, and carnivorous mammals score over hawks and owls, which rely on eyesight for hunting, in being able to follow scent trails and locate motionless or camouflaged prey.

Most of the climbing animals are small, agile creatures with tremendous balance which aids them in running and leaping from one swaying branch to another. All are adapted to cling tightly to the windswept canopy, for a 100-foot fall could be fatal. Squirrels, civets and martens have sharp claws that bite into the tree bark; monkeys have strong grasping hands and feet, and tree frogs adhere to the foliage by means of suckers on their feet. Some treetop animals have even attempted to rival the birds and bats by developing ingenious flying aids such as membranes of skin between their legs, webbed toes, or little flaps that can be erected like wings. Some, like several species of squirrels, can cover quite long distances through the air and can reasonably be described as gliding. Others make little more than extended jumps. Yet these antics are so unusual and remarkable that such arboreal creatures have traditionally been described as "flying". Borneo is famous for its flying fauna, and can boast not only of flying squirrels, but of flying lizards, frogs, and even snakes.

One of the most efficient "fliers" is the colugo or flying lemur, a curious creature about the size of a cat. The colugo has a loose, elastic skin membrane or patagium which extends like a blanket down both sides of its body, reaching from the chin to the tip of its tail and taking in the four limbs on the way. When the colugo jumps, it spreads the membrane like a large triangular kite and glides up to 150 yards to the next tree. Webs between its elongated fingers and toes increase its airworthiness.

I rarely saw colugos because they are extremely well camouflaged: their mottled grey coat merges imperceptibly into their normal background of bark and lichens. But I did see one female with her single offspring. Since colugos have no nest, the female carries the infant with her wherever she goes, while it grips her fur tightly. This mother was hanging upside down beneath a horizontal branch, her patagium forming a natural cradle for the baby.

Flying squirrels on the other hand are easy to see, and I had much pleasure watching the aerobatics of both large and small varieties. Like the colugo, flying squirrels have a patagium or flight membrane, but this does not include the tail, which streams behind them as they glide, helping them to steer. The red giant flying squirrels spend the daytime in holes in seraya trees, but I often saw them emerge in the late afternoon to bask and groom themselves in the fading sunshine before starting a night's feeding. As dusk came on they clambered to a high vantage point and launched themselves into the forest below. Once I saw squirrels glide as much as 200 yards over flat terrain from a tall durian tree, and in hilly country they can carry even farther. The steep vertical climb up the take-off tree is a cheap price to pay for the speed, ease, distance and directness of travel made possible by gliding.

Why then do only the nocturnal squirrels glide? The answer presumably is that the flight membrane impairs their running and climbing ability. Both the flying squirrels and the colugo appear awkward and clumsy in their climbing, and if they were active by day they would be vulnerable. They might evade mammalian predators by gliding to another tree, but they would easily be outmanoeuvred by any raptorial birds like hawks and eagles.

The last creatures one would expect to find flying are the reptiles, which would seem more at home crawling along the forest floor or slipping in and out of water. Yet in Borneo there are two quite different groups of flying lizard and no fewer than three species of flying snake. The golden flying snake, *Chrysopelea*, is a smooth-scaled, fast moving, tree snake. It is quite common and I saw it several times in the forest, but only twice did it oblige me with a flight. One sailed out of a low bush at an angle of 45 degrees and landed heavily on the ground in front of me. On another occasion a golden snake launched itself from a tall tree and landed in another some 15 feet away. For take-off the snake slithers quickly along a branch, gaining momentum, and shoots off the end, swimming through the air in a sigmoid curve. I would be inclined to call this leaping rather than gliding. The snake does, however, flatten itself as it leaps and draws in the ventral scales to form a hollow. This traps a cushion of air and gives the flier greater buoyancy.

Some lizards, on the other hand, are true gliders, and I got to know these quite well. The flying gecko, a small nocturnal species, was one of my favourite animals and for a long time I kept one as a pet. I had caught it in a butterfly net after spotting its mottled white shape on the trunk of a pale simpoh tree. It looked just like a miniature crocodile with big popping eyes and a permanent smile. Soon after I caught the animal I discovered that it had an amazing capacity to change its colour to suit whatever background it was placed against.

The gecko's ability to glide comes from its flattened shape and additional patagia. These flying surfaces are stiff flaps of skins which the gecko normally wears tight around its tummy like a waistcoat. When the animal makes its parachuting leap, the flaps are extended laterally to give lift. Geckos seem to glide only when they are disturbed, and it is possible that this trick has evolved as a means of escaping from potential predators, rather than for normal movement.

Unlike the little gecko, the flying lizard, *Draco*, clearly does use its gliding ability for travelling through the forest, and its skills are far more impressive. Several species of *Draco* are found in Borneo, and I often saw them clinging motionless and stick-like to tree trunks, watching for ants, which form their staple diet. Like other agamid lizards, *Draco* males are vigorously territorial. They chase off trespassers and reinforce their threats by frantic signalling with conspicuous, colourful throat flags This flap of skin varies from species to species: red, yellow, or sometimes black and white.

The flag is attached to a bony ray which can be spread open by muscular action. There is nothing unique about the erectile throat membrane; several other agamid lizards, including the common green *Calotes*, have it. But *Draco* is unique in having developed similar erectile membranes along its sides and neck. These lateral "wings" are supported by extensions of six of the animal's ribs—unlike the patagia of the gecko—and they enable *Draco* to perform amazing aerobatic feats.

I spent many hours attempting to record lizard flights on slow motion cine film, but the task was almost impossible. Before they launched themselves the lizards were hard to see, because, like the geckoes, they are designed to resemble bark and can even change colour to blend with different backgrounds. When airborne they displayed the bright red, purple or yellow spots on their flight membranes, and this might have made my job easier. But I never knew when *Draco* was going to leap, and once it did its movement was so sudden and its subsequent path so unpredictable that very rarely did I manage to capture the whole flight, from rapid take-off to gentle landing.

In a sense this was just as it should be, for *Draco* is designed to be startling. The sudden transformation from static drabness to active colour when it reveals its bright markings is intended to frighten predators. Moreover, the reverse transformation back to sudden inconspicuousness confuses the pursuer and makes it difficult to determine exactly where the *Draco* has alighted. I took heart from the knowledge that I was not alone in my frustration.

However adept *Draco* may be at arboreal living, the females are still compelled to make dangerous trips to the ground to lay their eggs. A sunny afternoon following a midday shower seems to be the favourite time for this activity, and I once saw several females laying at the same time. Each lizard dug a shallow hole in the ground where she deposited three or four oval, white, leathery eggs. As soon as she had finished laying, she hurriedly covered the precious deposit with the dug-up soil, scratching it back into the hole and hammering it firm with her head. Then she scurried back to the sanctuary of the nearest tree trunk.

Last but not least of Borneo's flying fauna is an amphibian: the elusive flying frog, first identified by Alfred Russel Wallace. It is a large species of *Rhacophorus*, the common tree frog, but its feet are greatly elongated so that the expanded webbing between the creature's toes acts like a parachute when it glides. Unlike most forest frogs which lay their eggs in semi-permanent puddles at certain times of the year—and suffer a heavy death rate from civets and monkeys—the tree frogs

The world's most efficient reptile aviator, the Draco or flying lizard, makes a spectacular glide between trees (right). Its unique, wing-like membranes, clearly visible in the artificial light of a flash, give sufficient buoyancy for glides of up to 50 feet, depending on take-off height. When it lands, Draco neatly folds its flight membranes along its flanks (above).

deposit their eggs in the tree canopy, within a rubbery mass of albumen which the females whip up into a froth with their hind feet. Each egg-mass is attached to the underside of a broad leaf or in some shady, humid spot in the lower canopy. Within this protective coating the tad-poles develop until a heavy shower washes them down into standing water, usually in tree holes, where they complete their metamorphosis. I once found one of these egg masses inside a camp storage tin that had been carelessly left open. It was a pink, sickly foam, rather like some exotic dessert, but the thought that it might easily have been mixed up in my food was rather unpleasant.

Nevertheless, after weeks of living in the rain forest, I had become more accustomed to unpleasant sights than I could have imagined before. Indeed, my whole outlook had changed radically. Things that had been important in the hubbub of Western life seemed utterly trivial in the tranquillity of the jungle, while other things normally taken for granted or not even thought about now took on a vital reality. Shelter from the rain, the comforting security of a familiar log or path, the loca-tion of drinking places, safe climbable trees for escape in case of danger, attention to tiny give-away sounds, the sharp appreciation of food: these were what mattered in the wilderness. I craved for salt and I craved for fat. Salt was easy to carry, but cans of meat were heavy and had to be severely rationed for my forest sorties. What really kept me going was the hope that when I got back to camp, the Dusuns might have killed a wild boar and we would be able to feast on its oily, red meat.

The Muslim inhabitants of Borneo will not touch pig meat but to many indigenous tribes of Borneo, including Ibans, Dusuns and Punans, the wild boar has been a source of meat for centuries. The hunting of it is a major part of their culture. Rather to my surprise, it also became an important part of my life. In some parts of Borneo blowpipes and ingenious traps are still used, but here on the Segama long broad-bladed spears were especially favoured for hunting pig. I joined in several of these expeditions and discovered the infectious excitement of the chase.

Sometimes the Dusuns lay in boats concealed at the river bank, wait-ing for migrating bands of pigs to cross the river. As soon as a party of old tusked boars, plump sows and striped youngsters plunged into the water to swim towards the far shore, the boats pushed out, the natives paddling wildly to cut off the herd and stabbing at the terrified beasts before they could reach the safety of dry land and the forest.

On other occasions two or three men set out on foot to pursue the wild boar in the forest. They were accompanied by their dogs, which would scent out, chase and corner the quarry, giving the hunters time to rush in with their spears and finish off the victim. I accompanied my Dusun helpers on such a trip. Our dogs ran on ahead and soon located a band of pigs. They barked frantically as they ran off in hot pursuit. We all hurried after the zig-zagging tumult. Suddenly the noise changed. Deep, bellowing roars warned us that the boars had turned on their yapping pursuers. The dogs baited their cornered victims, rushing in as the pigs turned, leaping aside to avoid the lunging tusks. We hurried up, panting.

The pigs turned to face this new, more serious threat. It was a dangerous moment: no time for cool reasoning, no time to worry whether the spear shaft would break or the blade bounce off the fierce tusks. Yelling and shrieking, we rushed straight in to plunge our spears into the quarry. For a few moments we were all wild savages. Only later, when the excitement had died down and we were cutting up the valuable carcases, did I realize how my legs smarted from many thorn tears and my bruised limbs ached from the exertion.

To have experienced such things is to have gone back far into man's past, to have discovered something of his primitive, natural role. How thin was the veneer of civilization, and how quickly had I accepted and enjoyed an activity that would have revolted me a few weeks before. On my first pig hunt I learned a great deal about my own nature. The cooperative hunt is exactly what man is designed for, both physically and emotionally. In the climax of the chase I found that all the senses and faculties of fitness, speed, courage and decisiveness were fully tested. Afterwards I felt closer to the forest.

Bluff and Double Bluff among Insects

Between the dim floor and sunlit canopy of the Bornean rain forest thrives one of the world's most diverse and ancient communities: a miniature, surreal world of insects and spiders. In a forest virtually unchanged for millions of years, they have responded to the pressures of evolution with an explosion of different species.

Innumerable permutations of colour, shape and behaviour enable them to exploit the thousands of varied homes available. At an optimistic estimate only 50 per cent of the forest floor species are known to science by name; as for the insect life of the canopy, even less is known.

Some of the most bizarre adaptations of colour and form have developed for purposes of camouflage. Every leaf and twig, flower and piece of forest rubbish is suspect. It may conceal, or even be, predator or prey. Vegetarian stick insects and leaf insects, for instance, are shaped and coloured for protection in perfect imitation of their namesakes, sometimes to the point of possessing diffuse patches of false rot or fungus.

Many crab spiders are coloured exactly the hue of a specific flower, while some praying mantises create an artificial blossom with their petal-shaped rear limbs. In this manner they not only avoid the predatory attentions of birds but also deceive their prey, flies and butterflies.

A few insects seem to find safety in looking like nothing in particular. Nondescript, bulbous larvae could be the earthy heaps left by worms, or fragments of fungus. Semi-transparent, circular little tortoise beetles simply merge with the world of light flashing through leaves and reflecting from drops of water, and they are easily overlooked.

In contrast, stark, bright colours serve to attract attention, often in order to advertise possession of an unpleasant taste or deadly poison. Such is the diversity of Bornean insect life that these deterrent hues may also be bluff: one unrelated, harmless species mimicking a dangerous one for self-protection.

Certain insects hold lurid markings in reserve to produce startling effects. Many moths have brilliant rings like large eyes concealed beneath their forewings and caterpillars posses similar markings on the front of their bodies. By making a sudden movement—a shuffle of the wings or a rearing of the head—these insects can frighten off a foraging lizard or an inquisitive bird.

The transparent thorax and wing cases of a tortoise beetle catch the light, almost concealing the brilliant gold of the body below. The combination of colours is a curiously indirect form of defence. At rest, the beetle looks like no more than a drop of water or a shiny patch on a leaf. In flight it becomes a ball of gold making a slow parabola from bush to bush. In neither guise does the beetle look like food.

On living plants above ground level, a bush cricket mimics green foliage.

Clinging to a twig, this bush cricket is camouflaged as a near-dead leaf.

A leaf grasshopper blends with the detritus of its forest floor habitat.

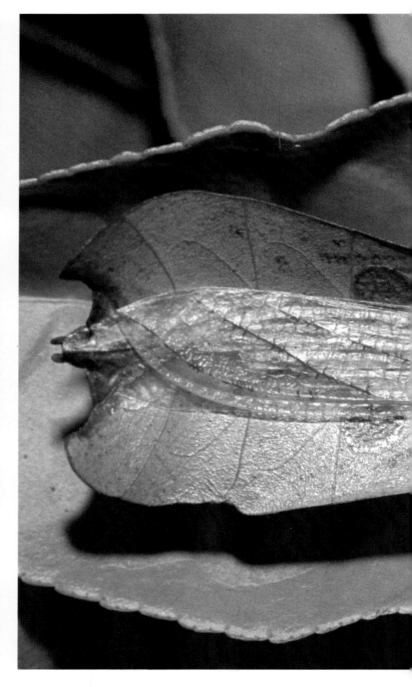

A pink-tinged leaf insect, inhabiting the upper vegetation level, appears to sprout from the very leaf of the plant it feeds upon.

The bright blue insignia and lurid pink flanks of the spiny Sertora caterpillar (above) are warning signs which predators would do well to observe. The caterpillar's turrets of hollow hairs can inject a powerful irritant poison, and a brush with these defences can be acutely painful.

Less dangerous but equally effectively coloured, a stink-bug nymph (right) advertises in shocking pink the fact that it has a bad taste. At the slightest disturbance the insect secretes a noxious fluid with a foul warning smell. Hopeful predators soon learn to shun insects with this distinctive livery.

A crab spider (above) crouches on its
white silk mat. Web and spider together
perfectly imitate the colour and
texture of a bird dropping. In this
disguise the spider not only conceals
itself from predators but also attracts
prey in the form of butterflies and
other insects that feed on excrement.

This false flower of the forest, the
Hymenopus mantis (right), spreads its
lower limbs and raised oval tail section
to imitate a spray of petals, tempting
butterflies to come and seek nectar. Its
front limbs, whose "elbow" joints can
be seen on either side of its head, are
poised motionless, ready to strike.

The striking false eye markings on the front of a hawk-moth caterpillar are part of a deterrent bluff. At rest these false eyes are concealed by a fold of skin. but when approached by a bird, the caterpillar rears towards it and the eyes are suddenly revealed. When faced with such a startling demonstration, most birds are scared off to seek their prey elsewhere.

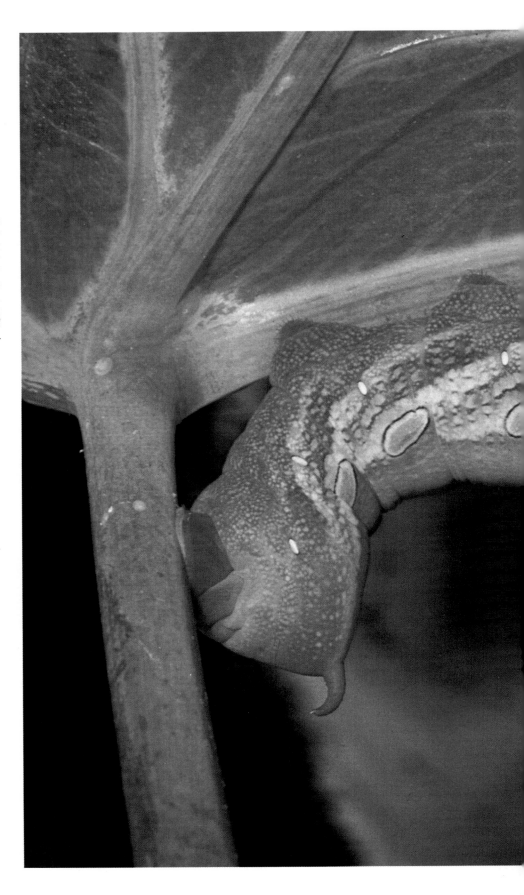

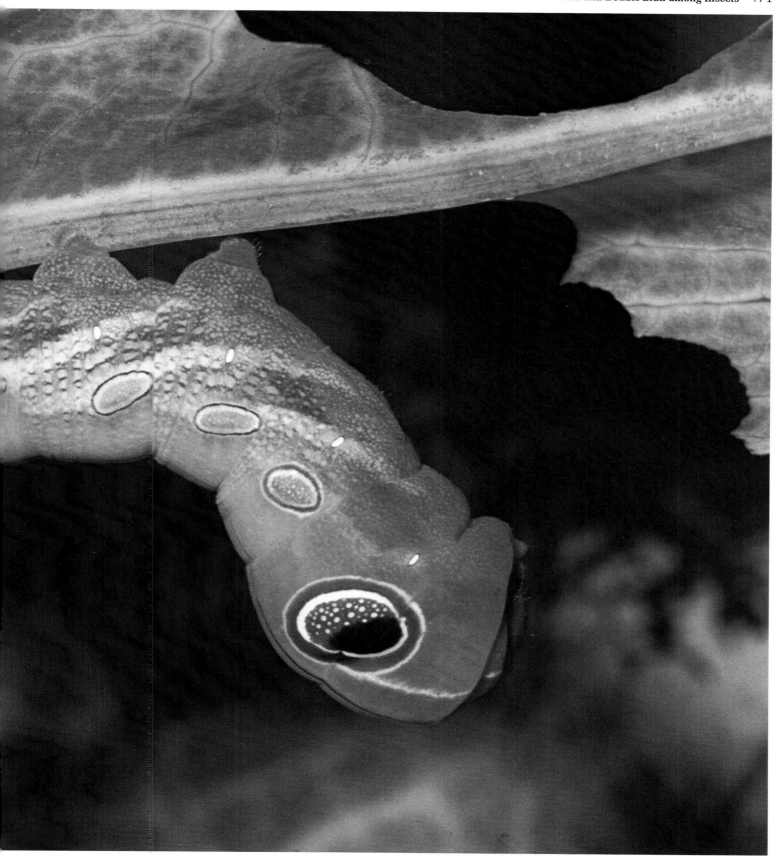

3/ Rungs to Man

Each has his own tree of ancestors, but at the top of all sits
Probably Arboreal; in all our veins
there run some minims of his old, wild, tree-top blood.

ROBERT LOUIS STEVENSON/ *MEMORIES AND PORTRAITS*

A century and a half ago, much of the Western world was in a state of uproar at the suggestion that man might be related to apes and monkeys. Yet the Bornean natives, without any sophisticated knowledge of evolution, have recognized a close link between man and apes. Many of the tribes regard the orang-utan, the red-haired ape of Borneo and Sumatra, as a spiritual cousin. One of their fables traces the descent of all orang-utans from a man who was ashamed of some misdeed in the village and fled to the forest, where by some strange metamorphosis he gradually turned into the first orang. Another story describes how bird-like deities created all the world's life forms. When they made man, the bird gods were so pleased with their handiwork that they held a great feast to celebrate. Next day, when they had recovered somewhat from their excesses, they tried to create more people but, alas, they had forgotten a vital ingredient and succeeded only in making orang-utans.

In fact, man is closely related not just to apes and monkeys, but to numerous other animals as well, including squirrel-like tree shrews, furry lorises and strange, staring tarsiers. All these mammals are usually classified as members of the most advanced order of the animal kingdom, the primates, and they can be identified by their possession of at least some of man's evolutionary advantages.

Primates are very well represented in Borneo. No fewer than 21 species are found on the island, including some of the most spectacular of all, such as the tarsier. But the special interest of the Bornean types is that they represent more rungs of the evolutionary ladder leading to man than do primates in any other part of the world. This is not to imply that they stand directly on the line to man: they do not. All the living primates have developed from evolutionary ancestors that are now extinct. They are offshoots of man's family tree. What I found fascinating about Borneo's primates is that they belong to grades of anatomical development and social organization very similar to those which man's ancestors must have passed through. By watching them in the forest around my camp, I felt I was glimpsing man's own far distant origins.

The extinct ancestors of the primates 70 million years ago were small, insignificant animals that lived on the ground, but thereafter primates became larger and mostly arboreal. Indeed, it was their various adaptations to tree life which distinguished their development. Their eyesight was improved at the expense of smell, and most primates have short noses and large, forward facing eyes like man's, which give them the binocular vision so essential for judging distances when leaping through trees. Hands and feet have shed the claws of more primitive creatures and have developed blunt-nailed, flesh-padded fingers for grabbing branches (and, ultimately, able to handle tools such as flints and axes). Most primates assume upright postures in many of their activities—a step towards the two-legged human form. They bear their young singly and give them prolonged post-natal care, as does man. Many groups have complex social organizations, foreshadowing human society, and primates as a whole are more intelligent than other mammals, a distinction which in man has made possible the development of language and other cultural accomplishments.

All this I was able to observe in Borneo. Above all I could watch the orang-utans. Modern zoologists now regard these rare apes as one of man's closest relatives, basing their conclusion on examination of bones and fossils and on biochemical comparisons of blood proteins and chromosomes. I had always been fascinated by the idea of these curious man-like creatures inhabiting remote jungles at the edge of the world, shrouded in legend and folklore. The behaviour of orang-utans is still very little known, either to the Bornean natives or to Western zoologists. Attempts to study them in the wild have always been frustrated by the inhospitability of the jungle and by their elusive, solitary life style. What I was able to see during my first three months up the Segama river only whetted my appetite for more, so I later made a second trip and spent long hours tracking them through the forest. In the process I discovered a good deal of new information about their behaviour, a story that deserves a chapter of its own. On both trips, of course, I built up a wealth of detail about more easily observed primates from many other rungs of our evolutionary ladder.

The bottom rung of the ladder is represented by the tree shrews, beautiful little creatures that scamper warily through the leaf litter on the forest floor, probing rotten logs with their sensitive snouts in search of juicy beetle larvae, crickets and fallen fruit. There are nine species in Borneo and they are all so squirrel-like in appearance that anyone could be forgiven for thinking that is what they are. The native people certainly regard them as squirrels and use the name *tupai*, meaning squirrel, for all the species. The English name, tree shrew, is no less confusing because actually they are not shrews and spend more time on the ground than in the trees.

Tree shrews have so many primitive features that zoologists are still arguing about whether they are primates at all. Their eyes are set back on either side of their long, foxy snouts and they do not have binocular vision. They have sharp claws rather than the blunt nails of other primates and they mark out the boundaries of their territories in a comparatively primitive way, using scent secreted from glands in their necks and groins. Moreover, they normally give birth to more than one offspring at a time. Like more advanced primates, on the other hand, the tree shrews sit upright to eat, holding their food in their hands; and they possess five fingers and the full primate complement of teeth. Whether accepted as true primates or not, they are certainly very similar to the primitive mammals from which the primate stock must have evolved.

Occasionally I saw two or more tree shrews disputing territories, squeaking loudly as they chased back and forth over their scent-marked boundaries. But they are not social animals, and I more often found them travelling alone, freezing at the slightest sound, sharp button eyes scanning the forest floor for danger. A flick of the bushy tail, a warning growl and the tree shrew was gone.

I was particularly intrigued by the tree shrews' odd reproductive behaviour. During breeding, a mated pair shares a leafy nest hole close to the ground, but the father plays no part in rearing the two or three offspring. Instead, the female makes a separate nursery nest in which to deposit her naked young. She herself visits the newborn infants only once every two days to suckle them, but her milk is so rich that they thrive on this infrequent feeding. It is almost as though she were trying to keep the existence of the new family secret from the father.

Only one type of tree shrew is nocturnal and it is sufficiently distinct in other respects to merit a genus of its own. The pen-tailed tree shrew was first described by that versatile amateur naturalist, Sir Hugh Low, who trapped one in the bungalow of the White Rajah, Sir James Brooke, while staying as his guest in Sarawak. That he should set mammal traps inside the rajah's house conjures up a pleasant picture of the life and attitudes of these early colonial dignitaries.

The pen-tailed tree shrew is far from common and, on account of its nocturnal habits, rarely seen. But one night I did get the chance to watch it by the yellow light of my torch. Two bright eyes flashed up and down among the dense vines in a patch of secondary growth near my camp. On closer inspection I could even see a curious stiff white brush at the tip of the animal's tail. Scientists have puzzled over the function of this unique development. In the dark jungle it is like a flag, and it is more than likely used as a social signal, just like the bushy tails that are waved by other tree shrews during the day.

A rather more advanced creature is the furry slow loris. Its name is partly derived from the Dutch word *loeris* meaning clown, and the description is certainly apt. With its big eyes, sweet face and quizzical expression, it looks just like a bemused comic. It is also incredibly slow. Like a mechanical toy in slow motion, the loris creeps slowly and carefully about the canopy, so quietly that it can steal up on a resting insect or dozing bird before its prey is aware of the danger. In a flash, a powerful hand reaches out, and the loris is happily crunching on another unfortunate victim.

Lorises are very shy animals and curl up into tight balls when disturbed. Rarely did I see more than a flash of eyes among the tree tops, a brief glimpse as the animal froze in my probing torchlight. On one occasion I was completely baffled because the eyes seemed to be flashing on and off. It was only afterwards, from watching lorises I kept as pets, that I realized what was happening. The animal was grooming himself. With painstaking care he licked every inch of his thick coat and at every bob of his head the eyes vanished from view. I should have been able to guess the explanation, for lorises are particularly fastidious creatures. To aid them in combing through their thick, soft fur they are equipped with a curious prong, or toilet claw, on the second toe of each hind foot. All their other fingers and toes conform to the typical primate pattern with blunt, monkey-like nails backing tacky pads.

Lorises have various other features that quell any doubts about their membership of the primate order. Unlike the tree shrews, they produce only a single young at a time, a tiny furry bundle that clings tightly to the fur on its mother's chest, suckling from the single pair of teats just like a baby monkey. They also have big eyes at the front of their heads. On the other hand they are quite clearly not in the same category as monkeys and apes, the higher primates. Lorises are nocturnal and use scent signals in much the same way as tree shrews to mark out their ranges. They are a comical sight as they clamber slowly and awkwardly along the branches of their main travel routes, dragging their bottoms over the bark and leaving streams of pungent urine in their wake. Another primitive feature of the slow loris is its nose, which is extremely moist like a dog's (monkeys and apes all have dry, hairy noses).

Such a clear distinguishing characteristic is exactly what the taxonomist seeks, and it would be convenient to take the dry nose as the main criterion for dividing primates into higher and lower types. Unfortunately, there is one exception, the tarsier, that upsets the neatness of this zoological classification.

One of the first things a zoologist notices about the tarsier is that it has a dry, hairy nose, and he might therefore think he had found a higher primate. But in other respects the tarsier is a quite primitive animal, a fluffy, six-inch goblin with a long tufted tail, a head too big for its body, large papery ears and enormous staring eyes. In relation to its body a tarsier's eyes are 150 times bigger than a man's; in fact they are considerably bigger in volume than its entire brain. They bulge out of their orbits to such an extent that a tarsier cannot give a glance, as we can, out of the corner of its eye. If it wants to see something on one side it has to turn its whole head, a manoeuvre it performs with the same unsettling ease, and for the same reasons, as an owl. It can, if necessary, swivel its head through 180 degrees and look directly backwards over its shoulder blades. The Dyaks believe that it can turn its head through a complete circle. The attachment of the head to the body is evidently, in their opinion, rather less secure than in other animals. Consequently, they used to believe that it was a very bad omen to encounter a tarsier when setting out on a head-hunting raid: in their estimation, the man who saw it would soon be losing his own head.

Tarsiers usually inhabit dense secondary forest, not because this is the best place for them to find food but because there are plenty of saplings and creepers, types of vegetation that suit their unique mode of travel. When they are on the move, they leap between vertical supports in an upright position in much the same way as a tree frog. Like a

A baby slow loris practises the tenacious grip that will enable it in adulthood to inch stealthily along slender branches in quest of insects, birds and small reptiles. Each of its forearms contains an extensive network of blood vessels that distributes the flow of blood evenly through the tissues and allows the muscles to remain tense without danger of getting cramp.

medieval gargoyle, the tarsier clings to a vertical branch with knees up and long, thin fingers gripping firmly, the circular pads at their tips giving extra adherence to the smooth bark. With a powerful kick from the strong back legs, it makes a spectacular leap, often covering six feet or more. In mid-air, the little acrobat twists round like an athlete on a trampoline as it manoeuvres towards another slippery upright, and then whips its tail over its head for balance when it lands. Strange though this method of travel may sound, it is very effective and has been in practice for 60 million years, ever since the earliest tarsiers gambolled in the primitive forests of Europe and North America.

Next on the evolutionary ladder are the monkeys, the first of the higher primates, and very much more advanced. They are far larger and live much longer than the lower primates. Their hands and feet are beautifully adapted for grasping everything from branches to insects. They are more intelligent, more adaptable and live in complex social systems. Instead of using scent trails, they designate the boundaries of their territory by aggressive behaviour.

I was aware of monkeys wherever I went in Borneo, along river banks, through lowland jungle or mountain forest, or in the fringing swamps of mangrove and nipah palms. If I did not actually see them, I heard them as they crashed away among the branches, uttering their harsh alarm calls. The two most widespread species were the pig-tailed and long-tailed macaques, respectively known as *berok* and *kera* after the sound of their calls. These are general, all-purpose monkeys, equally at home in the trees or on the ground, and they are opportunist feeders, taking fruit, leaves, flowers or insects. The two species are a superbly complementary pair. The *berok* is a large monkey, short and stocky with a curly apology of a tail; the *kera* is smaller, lean and slim with a long, flowing tail. The *berok* travels mainly on the ground, the *kera* leaps agilely among the trees. The *berok* is an animal of the hills, the *kera* is a resident of the river banks. Between them *berok* and *kera* just about cover the island, and the only monkey niches left vacant are filled by certain specialist leaf-eaters.

A group of 20 *kera* lived in the forest behind our camp and cheekily threatened us with glares and head bobs whenever we made so bold as to look at them. They never missed a fruiting fig tree and would crowd in to feed, jostling and squabbling until the branches sagged beneath their weight. Every day the troop set off on a foraging trip into the forest, travelling in a wide arc that brought them back to their sleeping trees by evening. In the gathering dusk, the youngsters squealed in play while their elders settled down for a quiet grooming session, their long tails dangling limply beneath them.

In Borneo there are five species of leaf-eating monkey, relatives of the Indian langur, and all are specialists in different types of forest. Near our camp we had three species: the red, the grey and the silvery. The red leaf monkeys were the most common and the most colourful, with bright red hair covering their athletic bodies and piled up round their blueish-black faces in comical crests. The rarer grey leaf monkeys were immaculate in neat grey coats, with white fronts and black hands and feet. Two black masking stripes blazed across their pink faces.

A group of charcoal-coloured silvery leaf monkeys occupied the river bank opposite us. They had two babies which fascinated me. Instead of sharing the subdued colouring of their parents, the infants wore coats of startling orange that stood out dramatically against their dark mothers and the shady vegetation. Such ostentation could draw the unwelcome attention of predators. But within monkey society it serves a very important function: it proclaims "here is a baby" and protects the nursing mother and her infant from aggressive members of their own species. Over about three months, the vivid orange coat fades through yellow, to pale straw and eventually to silver, so that by the time I left the Segama the infants were only slightly paler than their mothers.

Leaf monkeys are superbly agile animals and perform breathtaking feats of gymnastics as they leap from branch to branch and tree to tree. Like the tarsier, they use their long back legs to give them a powerful kick-off. While they are airborne, they swing their long tails round and round to maintain their balance. The leafy boughs bend to receive their weight, then spring back again when they bound gracefully away.

Leaf monkeys are far more arboreal than either of the macaques, and in Borneo I never saw one descend to the ground. But they must come down sometimes, since one of our dogs managed to catch a red leaf monkey and dragged his trophy back to camp, wagging his tail proudly. Here it was received eagerly by my Dusun helpers who immediately set about preparing it for dinner. Compared with some of the things I was invited to eat during my stay, monkey seemed quite acceptable, but my enthusiasm abated somewhat when I discovered the monkey's severed head grinning up at me from the yellow, oily stew.

Next to man on the evolutionary ladder are Borneo's two apes, the long-limbed gibbon and the hefty orang-utan, tail-less fruit-eaters with a much more upright posture than any of the monkeys. Unlike the

A huge-eyed tarsier snarls defensively, its black pupils reduced to mere spots in a patch of bright sunlight. With its superb vision and the alert sense of hearing provided by its broad, papery ears, the tarsier is able expertly to pinpoint the juicy crickets and beetles that it stalks by night.

elusive orang-utans, which are certainly the more intelligent of the two, the gibbons are very much in evidence. No one could fail to be impressed by their clamouring and their gay acrobatics as they weave through the shady canopy. Suspended by their long arms, they dangle beneath the branches and cartwheel along at amazing speed, launching themselves into space, and crossing from tree to tree in a series of daring leaps. A quick pause to scoop water from a tree-top crevice, a short rest to imbibe the liquid, and they are off again, patrolling their territories.

Unlike the group-living monkeys, gibbons have adopted the family as their basic unit, and some of their social problems seem recognizably human. Each family—usually a mated pair with two or three offspring— jealously guards its territory and engages in fierce battles with its neighbours if it suspects they are trespassing. Young bachelors who have moved out on their own are a source of constant friction. So long as they remain single, they are tolerated, in spite of the trouble they may cause in their attempts to wrench some territory of their own. But each day these lone males give a characteristic call, and occasionally a wandering female is tempted to investigate. If she is satisfied with the match, she joins the male and the new pair proclaim their partnership in a whooping duet. This is a testing moment, for the two of them may soon produce offspring and threaten the status quo. The established inhabitants attack in a furious attempt to break up the partnership, and usually succeed. But from time to time the youngsters manage to stave off the attack, or even retaliate, in which case they are able to consolidate a territory of their own and within a few days they are accepted into the gibbon established order.

Often as I lay half awake in the early morning I heard the start of the gibbon day. As soon as the first light filters greyly through the leafy canopy the male begins to hoot plaintively among the misty treetops. His call is more like the cry of a bird than that of a mammal—a sad whistling song heralding the dawn and rousing the daytime creatures from their nests and holes. Later, when the day has warmed up somewhat and the female has enjoyed a meal of figs, she joins her mate in an exuberant family chorus. Whoop after whoop rings round the forest as the whole family hoot their loudest to reach an ear-splitting climax. Suddenly the father and young fall silent, leaving the female gibbon to sing a solo. One long wail is followed by a shorter one and then another and another, steadily rising in pitch, faster and faster until the call erupts into a thrill of really joyful exuberance. For several seconds all is silent, and then the whole family start up again, repeating their dramatic performance, reiterating, as they do every day, that they are here, that this is their territory and they will defend it.

The morning chorus over, the gibbons spend the rest of their day travelling together round their family terrain. Like ghostly spectres they flit quickly and silently round their range, sampling the pick of the crop at the best fruit trees and munching on leaves and vines between whiles. At around four o'clock, when the monkeys are bestirring themselves from their afternoon rest to find their evening meal, the gibbon day is already over. Having fed well on rich fruit, the family retire to a tall tree and the animals spend the last few hours of daylight basking in the evening sunshine and grooming their thick woolly coats.

I found much resembling man in the gibbon, but the solitary orang-utan is as human as any animal could be. He is about the same size as a large man, he has an upright stance, an excellent memory and a propensity for "house" building. There were many of these man-like apes in the general area of my camp, and the opportunity to study them in the wild was too good to miss, especially as they are an endangered species. This was my reason for making a second trip up the Segama river. On my return here, I intended to establish makeshift shelters and caches of tinned food in the forest so that it would be easier to watch the orang-utans for several days at a stretch. Living in the forest could be a lonely existence at times, but so long as the orang-utans were around me in the forest, I felt I had company. In fact, I became quite closely involved in the lives of several individuals.

4/ The Private Lives of Orang-Utans

After the Rajah, the most interesting thing socially is the orang-utang. TOM HARRISSON/ *BORNEO JUNGLE*

Up in the tall merbau tree the great, shaggy red orang-utan shifted his position slightly and gazed up at the darkening sky. Black clouds scudded up from the south. The air was still and the insects and birds strangely silent. The ape had not seen me and he resumed his meal, breaking open the broad green pods and plucking expertly with his lips at the crunchy beans. I stayed where I was, squatting on a damp mossy log and peering at him through a tangle of foliage. Occasionally I turned away for a moment to glance at my watch and scribble a few words in my notebook under the heading Alexander, the name I had given to this individual. We both knew a storm was approaching. It might blow over as quickly as it had arrived or it might rage all night, shaking the tall trees and drenching the forest. We both hated storms.

The leaves began to stir and rustle, the first raindrops pattered on hard foliage and a growl of thunder echoed across the evening sky. I had spent the previous night in a nylon hammock slung between two trees but I did not fancy repeating the experience in the coming fury. I would wait to see where Alexander made his nest, then hurry back to camp, a mile away through the darkening jungle. Alex continued with his feasting, although by now heavy rain was beating on the obscene, swollen cheeks of his broad, ugly face. I pulled my cape over my head and wrapped my binoculars, for they were of no use in the sudden downpour. Flashes of lightning pierced the forest gloom and the tree-tops rocked crazily back and forth. A branch tore free and crashed heavily to the ground. Alexander stuck it out for another five minutes, then climbed laboriously down into a smaller tree nearby. I could hardly see him, but I knew from the sound of breaking branches that he was bending the boughs together to make a springy bed, his only shelter for the night. I left him to it and picked my way back to camp through the dark, wet forest, careful to avoid the many barbed rattan tendrils.

On my second trip up the Segama river I was still using the same base camp at the junction with the Bole river. Things had changed slightly, however. Camp had grown from a single open shelter to three small, stilted houses in a riverside clearing. I had two new Dusun helpers, Bahat the boatman and Pingas his assistant, who grew maize, tapioca and sweet potatoes. Rice was brought up regularly from the *kampong* but otherwise we needed few supplies. The rivers teemed with tasty, fat fish, and fresh meat was often on the menu after a successful pig or deer hunt. While the men tended camp I was free to work alone in the forest, keeping in touch with the many orang-utans which visited these parts.

Alex was a newcomer, but I had got to know him quite well. For several days before the storm, I had been tracking him through the forest, watching his every movement. I had first met him a couple of weeks earlier. One day I heard a male orang-utan issuing his characteristic call to the west of my camp and set out in search of him. A scattered trail of fresh feeding remains and newly built nests gave me the final clues to his whereabouts. I passed beneath him once without realizing it, but the strong smell of orang persuaded me to turn back. My diligence was rewarded. There was Alex peering over the rim of his springy couch of leaves, eyeing me suspiciously.

He was by no means as pleased to see me as I was to find him. Climbing to the top of a small tree, he shook it violently to and fro. When this did not send me away, he snapped off a couple of good-sized branches and tossed them to the forest floor. After this display of strength he sat back to watch my reactions. As I still made no move, he evidently decided I was harmless and climbed calmly away through the network of the forest canopy. I followed at a discreet distance, trying to remain out of sight, for I had no wish to upset him further.

I found that an unobtrusive method of following orang-utans was the only way I could keep in touch and study them without disrupting their normal habits. The results were immensely rewarding, for I was able to build up a detailed picture of their everyday life. Alex's daily routine, like that of the other orangs I tracked, was a leisurely mixture of travel and feeding, each snack followed by a rest. At dawn he left his nest and breakfasted in the tree that had provided his evening meal the day before. Then he usually took a brief rest before setting off slowly through the tree canopy in search of another fruiting tree. His method of travel was cautious and thoughtful. When he came to a gap he did not leap, but swayed his own tree backwards and forwards until it had swung far enough across for him to grab a branch of the next. He pulled the two crowns together, transferred his weight to the second, and moved across in safety. The mothers I saw travelling with their young employed the same technique but they remained suspended between two trees, providing a bridge for their offspring, before swinging over themselves.

Some 17 orang-utans resided in the vicinity of my camp and these I saw regularly from time to time. Alexander, however, was one of the many homeless nomads that wandered over enormous tracts of forest, either unwilling or unable to settle down within a fixed range. I never saw him with another orang-utan, either male or female, and he seemed to lead a very lonely life. This is the norm in orang society. Males almost invariably travel alone, and although adult females are often accompanied by one or two youngsters, they never join up with other mothers to form larger groups, as do the other higher primates.

There is a simple explanation for this solitary existence. Orang-utans are big animals with a specialized diet, and their main problem is finding food. Because of their weight they find travelling through the tree-tops difficult and can forage only over about a quarter of a mile a day. To compound the problem, their favourite species of fruit—figs, durians, rambutans, mangosteens—are rare and widely scattered. Consequently the population must split up. Orangs cannot afford to be too social.

Fruit usually was scarce in the forest, but occasionally there was a local superabundance of food. A huge ripening fig tree in my area attracted several of the resident apes over a period of three days. Red-beard, one of the resident males on my list, hardly left the feast and nested in the fig tree each night. Other regular visitors included four adult females with their offspring in tow. Good feeding sites like this were most exciting to watch, and I made myself a hide-out from which I could gain a rare view of the behaviour of several orang-utans together. I was amazed to discover that the diners showed a complete lack of interest in one another. Normally apart, they seemed to have lost all social arts. There was was no co-ordination in the timing of their feeding and resting, no tendency for animals to arrive or leave the tree together, and no mutual grooming, friendly greetings, or any of the other behaviour patterns that one might have expected. Only the young orang-utans enjoyed the company. While their mothers remained aloof the youngsters seized their chance to play rough and tumble games with others of their own size. Juveniles chased each other to and fro, swinging on lianas, grappling and biting. As soon as one showed signs of flagging, his partner prodded and poked until he was goaded back into life.

In spite of their lack of friendliness, the adults did not seem to object to the presence of the other animals. Redbeard made no attempt to molest any of the smaller orangs who came to harvest the figs. Nor did I find any evidence of jealousies between the females. But I never saw two fully grown males feeding peacefully side by side. Rivalry between males seemed to be intense. Only twice did I see two large male orang-utans together, and on each occasion the encounter erupted into a violent display, ending with the dominant animal chasing the other off.

Usually, males settled their disputes from a distance, bellowing forth long calls and challenging their rivals. A big male orang-utan displaying and calling is a truly formidable sight. Redbeard often gave voice, but the most regular caller in the neighbourhood was a bad-tempered old patriarch whom I had named Harold. Watching Harold, I could almost feel a calling display building up inside him. He became more and more violent in his feeding or travelling until he simply had to let off steam. His great throat pouch inflated, he wildly shook the tree he was in, raised his head and let out a long series of deep bubbling noises that gradually built up into a bellowing climax of throaty roars. Slowly the calls tailed off, with Harold bubbling as gently as at the start. These bouts could last up to three minutes and Harold sometimes called as many as five times a day.

The relationship between Harold and Redbeard was fascinating. Harold lived to the west and Redbeard to the east of a ridge marking the border between them. If there was no sign of Harold, Redbeard often delivered a barrage of calls from the ridge, all directed to the west. At other times Harold called from the border, bellowing his defiance eastwards. However, another patriarch, Raymond, ranged unconcernedly on either side of the line. Raymond did not visit the area often and he called very infrequently, but it was enough to keep both Harold and Redbeard at bay. Raymond's challenges were rather exceptional in that once he was in full cry he would raise his voice for a second, or even third climax. Possibly it was this show of excessive vigour that won him such respect among his rivals. They were certainly very shy of him and went out of their way to avoid a meeting. Raymond's calls carried as much as a mile through thick forest, so he was able to maintain exclusive rights over quite a large area when present. The others competed for similar territorial rights when he was absent.

The Dyaks have their own explanations for the calling of male orangs. They tell of one male who kidnapped a native girl from her village. He kept his captive in the trees and fed her wild fruits. Eventually she had a baby that was half man and half ape. One day when the ape was not looking, she wove a rope of coconut fibre, descended to the ground and ran off, clutching the child. Soon her captor noticed her absence and rushed in pursuit. The girl made for the river where a boat was just drawing away from the bank, but the orang-utan was nearly upon her. The boatmen shouted to her to drop the child. This she did and managed to reach the boat in safety while the distracted ape stopped to pick up the infant. Mad with rage, the orang-utan tore the baby in two, hurling the human half after the departing boat, and the ape half back into the jungle. The loud calls of the desolate orang-utan can still be heard as he wanders the forest in search of his lost bride.

Myth apart, the Bornean natives believe that the calling males are competing for females. At first I thought there was some truth in this. Each male usually claims an area that overlaps with the ranges of several adult females, and the calling male, therefore, seems to be the suitor most likely to benefit when females are receptive. In support of the theory, I saw females on two occasions who appeared to be attracted to a calling male. On the other hand, I also witnessed several incidents that suggested an opposite conclusion. Quite often I saw females actively avoid the big calling males and I frequently found females travelling in company with younger, non-calling males, whereas the big patriarchs travelled alone. I formed the impression that the calling males were no longer very much interested in females. One incident involving Harold rather confirmed this view.

Harold had spent the past three days on Central Ridge, as I named his border with Redbeard, and had called several times during his visit. He had just called again and, duty done, was sitting back resting in a vine-draped tree, gazing vacantly across the valley. Suddenly he became alert. I too could hear the unmistakeable noise of a heavy orang-utan crashing through the branches, heading up the hill straight towards the two of us. Harold watched carefully, then suddenly decided to act. He climbed down to the ground and slipped quickly away without a sound. I still could not see the newcomer but assumed from Harold's undigni-

Securely anchored by both feet and one hand, a young male orang-utan cautiously bridges the gap between two trees with his seven-foot arm-span. By pulling on the tip of the branch he has grabbed, he will draw the rest of the branch within reach, and thus gain a firm handhold with which to swing himself across. Heavy-bodied orangs prefer this mode of locomotion to the leaping of more light-weight apes.

fied retreat that it must be a big male, perhaps Raymond. I did not have to wait long. The new arrival climbed into the tree next to that so hastily vacated by Harold. Much to my surprise it was an adult female, closely followed by her juvenile son. Presumably she had been attracted by Harold's calls but he simply did not want to be involved.

A question I considered for a long time in view of this incident was why the male orangs should spend so much time calling. Were there other reasons apart from maintaining territorial integrity? And why it so important to them to keep their ranges to themselves? I came to the conclusion that their displays had certain important social functions. This may seem strange among animals that lead so solitary an existence, but it is likely that some sort of social relationship does exist between the different orang-utans that share the same areas. Possibly the calls of the most dominant males help to maintain contact among scattered families and individuals. When fruit is scarce or very local, the broadcasts of the elders may well help the less experienced animals by guiding them to the places where food can be found. In addition, the aggressive behaviour of the big males, which keeps out strangers and intruders, probably serves to protect their ranges against over-exploitation.

It was obvious that a close control of population was being exercised by orang-utans near my camp. I found significant differences between the community living to the north of the Segama river, my own side, and the other community on the south bank. In the southern population many of the males were consorting with females and breeding seemed to be in full swing. On the north side of the river, however, males called almost three times more often than their southern counterparts and were more aggressive. They rarely consorted with females and there were very few infants. Here breeding seemed to have come to a halt.

Usually it is difficult to relate cause to effect in wild populations of animals, but in this case there seemed to be an obvious explanation. While the southern forest was quite undisturbed by man, the forest to the north stretched to the heavily populated Kinabatangan river. There, timber companies had begun extensive felling operations and were working steadily south. The orang-utans' habitat was being continually eroded. It is my firm conclusion that the large number of apparently homeless, nomadic orang-utans I met north of the river were animals that had been forced to look for new ranges when their old haunts were destroyed. Because the Segama is a wide river, the refugees could not cross, and so only the northern population was affected. The dramatic drop in their reproductive activity suggests the existence of delicate behavioural mechanisms that regulate the birth rate in orang-utan populations to suit local or temporary conditions, something our own species might well be advised to investigate, if not to copy.

Although my time in Borneo was too short to follow any one individual all through its development, I was able to supplement my existing knowledge about orang-utans with numerous brief observations and so piece together a detailed picture of the animals' typical life histories.

Orang-utans may live up to the age of 40, and, as natural mortality is low, they do not need to breed very fast to maintain their numbers. Consequently, mothers can afford to lavish a lot of time and attention on each baby to give it the best chance of survival. Infants are not weaned until they are two years old and there is at least three years between births of successive young. From the age of eight when she reaches maturity, until her death, the female orang-utan is engaged in a constant cycle of child-bearing and rearing her young. As soon as one infant is weaned she becomes sexually receptive again and is joined by a male, usually sub-adult. Males take their family commitments lightly. After a brief courtship, lasting only a few days, or at the most a few weeks, they desert their mates, leaving them to raise any resulting young alone. Older infants and juveniles become very jealous when the mother starts to attract new suitors. Several times I saw youngsters attacking

A pregnant orang-utan hangs in a luxuriant strangling fig tree and scans the branches close above her for the ripest of the fruit.

much bigger males, hitting, biting and hair pulling in a pathetic attempt to keep mother to themselves.

For the first year of its life the infant orang-utan remains in almost constant contact with its mother, relying on her for food, transport and shelter. She is playmate, nursemaid and chief provider, and although she lets the baby taste her own food, at this stage the infant is still almost entirely dependent on her milk for nourishment.

As a youngster develops better co-ordination and control, it is allowed to play farther afield. It investigates branches, bending them together to form a little play nest, sitting inside and piling more twigs on top of its head. These early efforts are merely games, but such play is vital if the infant is to learn the important craft of nest building. If it is lucky, the baby orang-utan may have a permanent playmate, a juvenile sibling that is weaned but still travels with the mother.

Just such a family trio lived to the east of my camp. Joelle was accompanied by her two offspring: Joey, a rough and tumble juvenile male aged about five, and a baby who remained nameless because I was never able to determine its sex. Something about its face and demeanour made me think it a female, but it was such a woolly little thing I could never be sure. The infant still rode with its mother whenever the family travelled but could easily be tempted to join Joey in exciting games: swinging lianas, wrestling and biting, or chasing each other dizzily over and under a large horizontal branch.

Mother Joelle decided when and where the family went, although sometimes Joey would assert his independence and wander off alone for an hour or two while Joelle had her midday rest. Joelle chose the nesting tree each night and wove branches together busily while the youngsters played overhead. Her nest completed, she flopped wearily down and groomed herself diligently, waiting for dusk when the baby joined her. Joey always made his own smaller nest a few feet above his mother's. This was usually a last-minute affair built at dusk.

As the infants grow, their mothers become increasingly reluctant to carry them, and angry babies sometimes resort to noisy tantrums when they are forced to make their own way. The arrival of a new baby is an even more traumatic event. The elder sibling is suddenly forced into the juvenile stage of independence: it can no longer suckle, ride on mother or nest with her. The strong bond that existed between mother and offspring is weakened overnight. The mother will have little time now to devote to her ousted youngster.

As a juvenile, the orang-utan acquires the knowledge it needs in later life to feed itself. It learns the travel routes within its mother's range, memorizes the location and seasonality of the best food trees, experiments with the many forest fruits and leaves, and discovers what is edible and what must be avoided. Juvenile males seem more adventurous than their sisters, and wander off alone for longer and longer periods. Occasionally they may tag on to other family groups or gang up with other youngsters. Eventually they split away from their mothers entirely, dispersing over wide areas of forest in search of some gap in the mosaic of adult male territories where they can court suitable females undisturbed. Female young stay with their mothers until they are adolescent and attract suitors of their own. When they leave, they do not move far but take up residence on the edge of mother's range.

This long dependence on the mother is a sure sign of an intelligent animal, one that has to make conscious decisions based on experience rather than following fixed responses to certain stimuli. Indeed, one of the things that impressed me most about the orang-utans was their ability to master the complex problems of finding food. If they wandered randomly about the forest, they would find few of their favoured fruits. To survive, they must carefully plan the most economical travel routes and they must be able to predict with accuracy where food is likely to be found at different times of the year.

This is no easy matter in the complicated jigsaw of the rain forest canopy. Some trees fruit every few months, or even every few weeks; other trees bear a crop only every three or five years, a few even more rarely. To know which trees are going to fruit where, the orang-utan must rely on his long and accurate memory of past crop patterns. Even on a shorter time-scale, an orang-utan has to make some difficult calculations. He may know that a particular fig tree will last him for two or three more days, by which time a nearby durian tree he remembers from previous years should be ready. However, it may take him two days to cover the distance, with little to eat on the way. So he must decide either to stock up on extra figs for the journey, or plan a detour that will take in some edible vines or bamboo on the way.

I was amazed by the orangs' uncanny ability to turn up at the right place at the right time. A young male I called Humphrey entered my area during the durian season and I followed him on a well-planned trip which took us from one durian tree to the next. To my certain knowledge there were only 18 of these trees in the area and we visited six of them in one day. Humphrey had not been here for some time, and it was obvious he was using his memory of past years to check up on all the durians now that it was time for them to fruit. On another occasion, a female and juvenile were travelling slowly along a ridge when they discovered a merbau tree with big ripe pods. After feeding they headed down into the valley, straight to another merbau, also laden with pods, but not visible from the hill. Here they took their fill before clambering back up to the ridge and continuing their journey. They had clearly decided that as the first merbau was in fruit it was worth making a detour to investigate another nearby tree they knew of.

During the winter monsoon when cold, wet weather makes fruit scarce, orang-utans change their diet. They eat vines and the inner bark of various trees, and, if pushed, they can draw on the reserves of fat they have built up during the summer months of plenty. Nor do they disdain animal food, occasionally raiding ant and termite nests and devouring both soil and inhabitants with great gusto. I have even seen them poking about in tree holes, searching for birds' nests or squirrel dreys.

One food source that orang-utans rarely find but favour above all else are the great pendulous combs of the large, wild honey bees. The bees' nests are usually built under the branches of the tall mengaris trees that tower above the forest canopy. Mengaris trees rarely support lianas, and their smooth broad trunks offer no holds for an orang-utan to climb. But once I had the luck to watch a determined big male clamber into the crown of a mengaris from a convenient adjacent tree. He seated himself on a stout branch and set to work on a honeycomb. Immediately a cloud of fierce black bees enveloped the raider, but he was in no way deterred. Either his long hair and thick skin protected him or his love of honey was too great to be put off by a few stings. Unhurriedly the big ape continued his feasting, breaking off large handfuls of juicy comb and swallowing them; wax, grubs, honey and all. His only concessions to his persistent attackers were to close his eyes against their onslaughts, and now and again to grunt and wave his arm in front of his face in a feeble attempt to clear the buzzing swarm.

The orangs I had become so involved with were among only a few thousand that survive in scattered pockets in Borneo and north Sumatra. Once, these apes thrived throughout the great forests that stretched from southern China to Java. The reason for their decline in numbers is simple—man. Man and orang-utan are quite incompatible neighbours. Both require the same lowland forest—the orang to feed from and live in, and man to clear for timber and cultivation. Both compete for the same fruits: durian, rambutans, mangosteens. In addition, man has a long tradition of hunting the orang-utan for food. Charred bones found in the Niah caves in Sarawak testify to the ape-eating habits of early man nearly 40,000 years ago, and some Dyak tribes still enjoy orang meat today. Wherever man has moved into the forest, the orang-utan has fled: large timber companies are now felling the trees at an unprecedented rate and the habitat of the orang-utan shrinks visibly every year. To preserve the orang population, parts of the animals' ranges have been declared nature reserves. It is illegal to kill, capture, sell or export orang-utans from Borneo.

One of the most ambitious and intriguing programmes for conserving the orang-utan is rehabilitation. The idea, which was originally tried out by Barbara Harrisson, wife of Tom Harrisson, the energetic curator of the Sarawak Museum, involves trying to return to the wild those young animals which have been confiscated from towns and *kampong* where people had kept them as pets. This is not as easy as it sounds, but a systematic attempt to put the idea into practice is now being made by the Sabah Game Department at Sepilok, and a similar scheme is being run in Kalimantan at Tanjong Puting. Rehabilitation is necessary because the orphan apes have become accustomed to human contact and have missed the vital experience of spending their early years in the wild. Some cling tenaciously to their human custodians and are terrified of the forest; others do not know how to make proper sleeping nests. Most find the easy living around houses and fruit plantations preferable to the discomforts of their natural environment.

But there have been some successes, and a few animals have returned to the wild. One of the most optimistic experiences concerns Joan, an adult female at Sepilok. On one of her trips into the forest, Joan became pregnant by a wild male and to everyone's delight gave birth at the station to a baby, Joanne. When I first saw Joanne she was still a wobbly little thing, completely dependent on her mother, but by the time I left Borneo, she had grown up a proper little orang-utan girl, half tame, half wild. At the age of three, Joanne left her mother during a jungle foray to fend for herself in the forest. I hope she made it.

NATURE WALK / Up Mount Kinabalu

TEXT BY DAVID ATTENBOROUGH

PHOTOGRAPHS BY CLAIRE AND BILL LEIMBACH

Mount Kinabalu dominates northern Borneo. From the coast you can see it most mornings, 30 miles inland, an immense rectangular battlement jutting nearly 13,500 feet into the sky, its top castellated with towers and spires. It is not quite the shape it appears from below, but a J-shaped ridge with its main limb pointing northwards and the curl to the south enclosing a great abyss 5,000 feet deep.

The mountain is stocked with a phenomenal number of different plants. Some 72 genera of orchid have been recognised and collected, for example, and there are probably several hundred species blooming unnamed among the still unexplored gullies and ridges.

The first man to climb the mountain and record the event was Hugh Low, the British Colonial Secretary on the islet of Labuan and a passionate amateur botanist. In February, 1851, he was on his way "to deal with", as he put it, "some Bolanini pirates who had recently ravaged the coast". That problem, however, was not so urgent that he could not spare a couple of weeks to investigate the unknown mountain.

He marched inland for several days with 40 or so porters. He also took a guide armed with a large basket of quartz crystals and teeth to protect the party from the supernatural beings that dwelt on the summit. None of the Dusun people who accompanied him had ever climbed the mountain before, believing it to be the dwelling place of the spirits of their dead.

After what he described as "the most toilsome walk I have ever experienced"—a formidable indictment from such an energetic traveller— he reached the top. At least, he reached the summit plateau. He did not, it seems, stand on the peak that now bears his name, for he wrote, with a little dramatic licence, that "the highest point is inaccessible to any but winged animals". On the crest of the ridge he took out a bottle of Madeira wine and drank Queen Victoria's health. Then he wrote his name on a piece of paper, put it in the empty bottle and left it there, upturned. His porters watched this proceeding with interest and concluded, not unnaturally, that it was some kind of religious ritual. For years afterwards they insisted that any European who went up the mountain should do the same thing to protect the party from disaster.

Low's route, in its upper part, was

THE DAMP MOSSY FOREST AT 6,000 FEET

the one taken by botanists and ornithologists who followed him in subsequent decades and it is still, broadly, the one followed today. I climbed the trail after several months in the low country and it was like entering another world. The jungle above 6,000 feet or so was a totally different place, with hardly a species in common.

Here there were Castanopsis trees like Spanish chestnuts, Eugenias belonging to the myrtle family, and arching filigree tree ferns. Some of the taller trees were bearded with yellowish moss. Lycopodium, a club moss more akin to a fern than a true moss, straggled along the damp ground and another closely related species spiralled up tree trunks, drooping pallid elongated fronds. A tree with similar scale-like leaves clustering around its twigs seemed to be a third and giant Lycopodium species, but my companion George Mikil, the Senior Park Ranger and an expert on Kinabalu's flora, corrected me. It was a *Dacrydium gibbsae*, not a club moss, but a conifer.

The trail wound up through a world of pale greens, browns and greys, muted with mist which blew raggedly through the gnarled trees. For a moment the sun shone weakly through, but it was the last we saw of it that day. The mist thickened and began to condense into heavy drops which agitated the leaves, so that I thought a bird or lizard was moving in the undergrowth. As we plodded upwards, the rain strengthened and became drenching. George Mikil smiled tolerantly at my dis-

THE PITCHER OF NEPENTHES VILLOSA

LOW'S PITCHER PLANT

comfort. This was typical mountain weather and he was used to it.

It was here that we saw the first of the mountain's most famous specialties, a pitcher plant, found throughout South-East Asia, but nowhere in such variety as on Kinabalu. This one sprawled over a tree, dangling its pitchers in the air. Each pitcher is, in origin, a leaf tip which has become modified into a deep pot partly filled with fluid. Insects of all kinds are attracted by its scent. When they settle on its lip, they cannot maintain a foothold on the slippery waxy surface and fall into the liquid where they are dissolved and digested by the plant.

No less than seven species are known to grow on the mountain and there may be more. This one was *Nepenthes lowii*. Its pitchers are magnificently baroque, with a swelling belly, a tightly nipped-in waist and an extravagantly flaring lip. It was discovered by Hugh Low on his first ascent and named after him by that redoubtable Victorian botanist, Sir Joseph Hooker. (At the end of his scientific Latin description of the pitchers, Hooker added a sentence that is as splendidly evocative of his personality as of the plant. "A very elegant claret jug," he wrote, "might be made of this shape.")

Pitchers are usually green, patterned with red or purple. These we had found, however, were a glossy leather-brown. They were dead, killed by a recent drought.

Only a few yards farther on, we found another of Low's discoveries, *Nepenthes villosa*. This had survived the drought unharmed. The bellies of its pitchers were flushed pink and their lips glinted seductively with nectar.

New Sounds in the Forest

The continuing rain and increasing altitude changed the sounds of the forest. When we started, cicadas had been shrilling their tiny engines and from a distant ridge I had heard the long, low warble of a mountain barbet. Now, through the thrumming of the rain came the metallic piping of tiny frogs hidden somewhere in the moss. Perhaps it was the prospect of catching a frog that brought out a rat snake, which suddenly appeared in the Lycopodium, bobbing its head inquisitively among the vertical stems. It had big lustrous eyes and a brown body shading to crimson around its neck and chin. In my experience, most snakes, even the most venomous, are more than anxious to get out of the way of humans. This one, however, seemed quite untroubled by our presence

A MOUNTAIN BLACKBIRD

and watched us for some minutes before diving away.

Many of Kinabalu's animals display this sort of fearlessness. We soon saw another, even more striking example. A mountain blackbird, not unlike a European blackbird in appearance, except for an ochre-red patch on its breast, eyed us as we approached but did not fly away. Instead it busied itself in bushes no more than a few feet from us. In 1888, when naturalists were prone to kill everything on sight in order to establish scientific identity, John Whitehead, the first committed orni-

INQUISITIVE RAT SNAKE

thologist to climb the mountain, discovered a charming little warbler which ran around his feet more like a mouse than a bird. It was such a friendly and trusting creature that he had great difficulty in getting far enough away to shoot it without blowing it to bits. The Kinabalu friendly warbler is still tame (despite this encounter) and is one of several species found nowhere else, except here and on the neighbouring mountain of Trus Madi.

By the early afternoon we were approaching an altitude of about 9,000 feet. The vegetation was now little more than a few feet above our

COELOGYNE ORCHID

heads, with Leptospermum, a small-leaved shrub of the myrtle family, related to the tea-tree of Australia, the dominating plant.

Plants of the Higher Levels

The orchids we found were small, many of them epiphytes clinging to tree trunks and producing tiny stems of unspectacular flowers, the more charming for their modesty. The most conspicuous was at ground level, a pure white Coelogyne, arching its stem of blossoms among the sodden mosses. A fine species of scarlet rhododendron grew nearby.

In addition, a quite remarkable conifer had appeared in considerable numbers—Phyllocladus, the celery pine. It hardly looks like a conifer for, instead of needles, it has strange stiff spreading leaves, which in a strict botanical sense are not leaves at all but stems. The true leaves drop off while the plant is a seedling and never grow again. Lest

this definition should appear to be mere botanical pedantry, the adult Phyllocladus demonstrates the true nature of its greenery by producing its fruit directly from the rim of the apparent leaf. This plant, like so many on Kinabalu, has odd geographical connections—related species are found only in the Philippines, Tasmania and New Zealand.

BULBOPHYLLUM ORCHID

A TALL RHODODENDRON

Suddenly my attention was distracted from the flora by a plump rat which trotted out of the bushes across our path. It stopped, looked at me in mild astonishment for a moment, then continued its journey at exactly the same pace.

There are 18 species of rat in Borneo and at least six of them live on Kinabalu. As you might expect by now, one of them, *Rattus baluensis*, is found nowhere else. I could not tell whether the individual that crossed my path belonged to that species, but I doubt if even such zoological distinction would have been sufficient to quell my unscientific distaste for rats in general, even if, like this one, they live in the forest, independent of man and his food supplies. I was only grateful that it wasn't *Rattus infraluteus*, the giant mountain rat, which grows to a length of nearly a foot, not including its tail.

The rain, which had let up for about 15 minutes, started again even more heavily. We trudged upwards, acutely conscious of the precise moment when yet another part of our clothing finally succumbed to the drenching and another sodden cold patch made itself felt on our flesh. Around mid-afternoon, somewhere over 10,000 feet, we arrived at the small hut where we were going to spend the night.

It was not the snug, warm-timbered, Alpine-style hut with deep bunks and a roaring open fire that my imagination had fondly dwelt upon during the colder and more wretched parts of the day. It was made of chilly aluminium and the bunks were hard boards on metal frames; but it was waterproof and windproof, and at one end stood a cast-iron stove by the side of which the last occupant had thoughtfully left a pile of dry wood. The stove was soon burning, smokily but warm.

BUSHY VEGETATION AT 10,000 FEET

THE NAKED FLANK OF THE MOUNTAIN

path, had turned it into a waterfall. Our boots had long since filled with water, so there was no point in trying to keep our feet dry. Had we tried to do so by leaving the path and walking through the bushes we would have fared little better, for water was also gurgling through the knotted roots and sodden mosses.

It seemed astonishing that plants could maintain a hold on the rock in the face of such an onslaught by water, yet even the smallest crack in the granite seemed to be a niche for some plant—a lichen, a moss, or yet another species of Lycopodium.

That evening we were given a Kinabalu sunset. Sunsets at altitude have a special quality, for as the sun drops below the rim of the world, it sinks so far beneath you that its rays strike upwards and illuminate from below the banks of clouds that so often lie in the valleys beneath. This night, the heavy rain-laden clouds were lit in such a fashion by a theatrically sullen crimson glare. As the sun sank still farther, its rays faded from all except a few wisps of cloud that floated above the

While we were gathering more firewood outside, to keep the stove going through the night, the rain stopped and the clouds blew first into tatters and then into rents big enough to give us a glimpse of the upper mountain for the first time since we had been on its slopes. High above reared a vast naked flank of silver grey rock, like the glistening side of a whale breaching the surface of the sea, white-striped with water-falls roaring and glissading down the sheer face.

Although the rain had completely stopped, merely walking through the ten-foot high vegetation drenched us, for all the leaves and branches were loaded with moisture. Among the Leptospermum grew lower Schima bushes. Their shoots, a delicate purple and rimmed with pearls of water, were as beautiful as flowers.

The rainwater, sluicing down the

LEAVES OF A SCHIMA BUSH

LYCOPODIUM, A CLUB MOSS

clearly silhouetted outline of Mount Kinabalu. They, alone in the darkening landscape, were illuminated, like fumes hanging over the mouth of a furnace and catching the glow of invisible fires.

The Second Day

We rose at four o'clock next morning, determined to get high up the mountain before the clouds closed in. Below us we could see Kota Kinabalu, capital of Sabah, as a cluster of lights rimming the just discernible coast. Above, every star in the hemisphere seemed to be shining and the moon, a slim crescent, lay on its side as if in a hammock slung between the silhouetted spires of the eastern arm of the mountain. The view was blotted out in minutes, for the path took us into thick bush. In any case, we needed to keep our eyes on the beams of our torches to find footholds as the track steep-

ened. By the first light of dawn, we were clambering over naked rock.

It might be supposed that such an immense peak is the core of the island, an ancient nucleus from which other more recent rocks have been stripped by the forces of erosion acting over millions of years. In fact the reverse is true. Kinabalu is a relatively new arrival in the landscape, younger, not older, than the rocks that surround it, a great dome that welled up from the depths, forcing its way through the sandstones and mudstones that form this part of Borneo, cracking and pushing them aside like a shoot from a bulb breaking through the crust

of frozen soil in the early spring.

This cataclysmic event occurred a mere nine million years ago, and there is evidence that molten rock was still rising within Kinabalu only one and a half million years ago. What is more, according to the research of a team of Japanese geologists, the mountain is still rising at a rate of five millimetres a year.

Kinabalu's granite is beautiful rock, white felspars bespangled with long glittering crystals of black hornblende. In one place, we found a dark mass the size of a football. This was evidence that not much of the granite had been eroded away, for it was the metamorphosed re-

CLOUDS THEATRICALLY LIT AT SUNSET

mains of the rocks that had once overlain the intrusion and had melted and mixed with the magma.

The rocks we were crossing bore dramatic indications of the mountain's recent history. A deeply scored groove ran directly down the slope, over a hump and down a steep face. Its route and the hardness of the granite made it impossible to believe that it had been formed by water. It was a surface feature only, and there was only one agent that could have produced it—ice. Kinabalu was once crowned by glaciers.

Signs of Kinabalu's Past

It is not, perhaps, so extraordinary. Ice today does occasionally form in rock pools on the summit and from research elsewhere in the tropics it seems that it would only require a drop in the average temperature of about two degrees Centigrade to bring back permanent snow and, in due course, icefields.

The groove we found had been produced by a boulder frozen solid on the underside of the glacier which had cut its way across the surface of the rock like the tooth of a rasp.

METAMORPHOSED ROCK IN GRANITE

GREAT PLATES OF GRANITE

Glaciation probably came to an end about 34,000 years ago, leaving the rounded, smoothed surface of the mountain almost clean of debris. Since then, heating during the day and cooling to freezing point at night has caused the outer shell of the granite to split along lines of weakness, running parallel to the domed shape of the intrusion like the skins of an onion. These were formed when the molten granite hardened against the old sedimentary rock. Thus great plates and shields of granite, a foot or so thick, lie on the surface of the rock slopes.

The highest of the peaks rising

LOOKING INTO LOW'S GULLY

from the summit plateau is named after Hugh Low, and the next highest after Spenser St. John, the British consul in Sarawak who made the second ascent of the mountain, with Low, in 1858. Both men, perhaps, may be reckoned to have earned their immortality. The other peaks are labelled rather unimaginatively, and the two most spectacular, which jut vertically into the sky, have acquired the banal, slightly comic name of Donkey's Ears. I could not help reflecting that local Dusun names would have been far more appropriate and musical, like the word Kinabalu itself, which is almost certainly of Dusun origin and means "dwelling place of the dead".

The sun rose behind the Donkey's Ears, casting huge shadows across the granite slopes. We clambered on, warmer now, towards the crest of the ridge, and soon found ourselves looking down into the abyss in the

curl of Kinabalu's J. This awesome rent in the mountain is now known as Low's Gully, a hardly appropriate description since it is far more than a gully. The distance between where we stood and the eastern ridge of the mountain was about half a mile. In fact the gully that Low described and that later explorers, including St. John and Whitehead, clambered up and called by his name, seems to have been a relatively small feature on the southern slopes, probably somewhere below the Donkey's Ears. Someone later misapplied the name to the northern abyss. Maybe sometime it will be re-named. Low himself, I guess, would not have minded it being changed: he already has named after him a peak, a bird, a squirrel, a wild cow, a rhododendron, a buttercup, a raspberry and the jug-shaped pitcher-plant.

This abyss was also heavily sculpted by the glaciers that had formed

THE DONKEY'S EARS

a hanging valley immediately below us, and rasped into a smooth saddle a rocky spur that projects from the face 300 feet lower down.

No one has yet climbed into this secret and awe-inspiring place, although several attempts have been made. George Mikil is one of the few people who have travelled through the jungle in the north, and as we sat eating a breakfast of chocolate, he pointed out to me where he had been, the peaks he had climbed, and told me of his conviction that this was one of the very few places in the whole of Borneo where the rhinoceros still survives.

The summit is a place of such splendour that we stayed there as long as we could, wandering first to the base of the Donkey's Ears, then way over to the north-west where there were other summits shaped like turrets and horns. They were several hundred feet high, with sides which in places were either vertical or overhanging and which terminated in piles of cracked and riven boulders, quite unlike the unlittered lower slopes. These peaks must have been projecting above the icefields, or else so lightly covered in snow that they were eroded by the action of frost rather than the glacial ice which chamfered their flanks.

Pools of crystal rainwater had accumulated in the hollows in the granite, marvellously clean-tasting when we lay down to drink from them. There were no signs of life in the rock pools, or birds in the sky, but the place was not totally lifeless. A minute spider huddled in an angle

GRASSES AROUND A POOL OF RAINWATER

A DWARF LEPTOSPERMUM

TWISTED ROOTS IN A GRANITE CRACK

of a rock and by its presence indicated that there must be insects around to provide it with food.

Dwarf Species of Flowers

Where a corner or crack had trapped blown dust, tiny plants grew, crouching close to the granite —a yellow-flowered cinquefoil, *Potentilla leuccnota*, a dwarf Leptospermum only a few inches high but closely related to the species 2,000 feet below that grows to a height of at least 15 feet, and a small clump of what looked to my European eyes to be heather, each stem topped with tiny red trumpets. It was, in fact, a dwarf rhododendron.

The flora of the higher, more temperate parts of the mountain and the geological development of the area together form a jigsaw which, if we were knowledgeable enough, would reveal a detailed picture of the history of this part of Borneo. At the moment, however, the two together seem to raise more questions than they answer.

The plants have the most various

connections. To find the relatives of some we have to go to Indochina, of others to Ceylon and the eastern side of the Pacific. Most are found south of the equator in the mountains of New Guinea and Australia. Nearly all these localities are separated from Kinabalu by distances so immense that it seems impossible that they could be crossed by blown spores or seeds. Neither these plants nor their relatives seem to have been able to live in the hot, humid jungle on the land masses in between. How, therefore, were they transmitted

RHODODENDRON ERICOIDES

from one place to the other?

The question might be the more easily answered if Kinabalu were an extremely ancient mountain which could have provided a sanctuary for species surviving from an older and colder geological period. But now we know that, at nine million years old, it is one of the newest granite peaks in the world. Furthermore, evidence elsewhere in Borneo suggests that the jungle on the island has remained virtually unchanged for millions of years.

Perhaps mountains once linked the various places where these cold climate plants lived, and they have now been eroded away, leaving Kinabalu as the most recent but also the last, isolated refuge of the far-scattered plants. If there were, no one has found any signs of them.

There is a very long way to go before we properly understand the development of this part of South-East Asia and the manner in which its animals and plants have evolved and spread, disappeared or flourished; but it is more than likely that many of the clues to those secrets are to be found on this extraordinary and unique mountain.

We climbed to the very summit of Low's Peak, 13,455 feet high. Before Low went up, few if any Dusuns had been here because of their beliefs about the mountain. There were, of course, many legends about what was at the top. Low was told that there was a dragon guarding an immense jewel, and that the top was strewn with enormous grey pearls that no man dared touch, for to do so would flood the world below. Perhaps this last legend, which has been recorded independently since, is a reference to the rare showers of hail which occur at high altitudes—in which case it suggests that someone must have ventured quite close to the summit.

Later travellers were told that the top was covered by a lake on which floated many boats, each carrying a light, and that the spirits lived on mushrooms and tended herds of ghostly buffalo.

This belief in the supernatural power of Kinabalu continued for many years. Until recently expeditions going up the mountain had to specify in the agreements they made for porters, the precise size of the sacrifices they would make. The standard requirement was two fowls and seven eggs, given as offerings at the outset, two gunshots to warn the spirits of the impending invasion soon afterwards and a further two shots discharged in a northerly direction when the summit was

reached. Even today, only a few Dusuns regularly visit the summit, as porters. One of our companions on this occasion was Gindai, a local Dusun. He had often carried loads up to the top hut but, until we asked him to come all the way to the summit with us, he had never visited it. Whether this was because he had some dread of the place, I was unable to discover. There was little doubt, however, that as he looked about him, wide-eyed, he was as impressed by the scenery as I was.

Borneo lay spread beneath us: the coast away to the west; Mount Trus Madi, our nearest rival, 30 miles to the south; lines of unnamed peaks in the Crocker range away to the north-east; and between them all the flat hazy-green blanket of the jungle.

But it was to Low's Gully that we returned for the finest and most dramatic views. It was now nine o'clock in the morning and we knew it would not be long before the gully would be enveloped in cloud. Indeed, as we watched, clouds began to generate down in its depths. They came racing up so fast that at one moment the peaks of the east ridge were shining in the sun and the next they were invisible behind a maelstrom of mist.

We sat watching for an hour before a gust of rain gave warning that the clouds had closed for the last time that day. It was time for us to leave. Even before we got back to the vegetation line, the rain was torrential and the flanks of the great mountain were once again being sluiced clean by wide waterfalls.

THE VIEW FROM THE TOP OF KINABALU

5/ The Sacred Birds

"I am the ruler of the spirit world," said Singalang Burong, "and have the power to make men successful. In all the work you undertake you must pay heed to the voices of the sacred birds." IBAN MYTH

It was a curious looking bird, one I had never seen before: brown with a white collar and a ludicrous long dark crest which it raised and lowered constantly as though unable to decide which was the right position. The bird was not at all afraid of me and flitted from perch to perch only a few feet above my head. It studied me closely and chattered excitedly. I could not help feeling it was trying to tell me something. Nor, I later discovered, was I alone in having this reaction. Perhaps because it is naturally curious and noisy, the crested jay is one of the birds whose patterns of behaviour are regarded as omens in Borneo. Its call is an auspicious sign when fields are cleared for planting. Its appearance on a jungle trail in the days of head hunting was a good portent for a warring party, to whom its crest signified the hair tufts of beheaded victims.

My genial boatman, Bahat, was an authority on bird omens, a complex subject requiring detailed observation, and during the time I spent with him in the jungle I learned much about the birds of Borneo, their roles in native religion and mythology and their behaviour in the rain forest. Bird augury is deeply rooted in the jungle way of life, and I had to accustom myself to the fact that if the Dusuns in my employ heard the descending notes of the Diard's trogon or met a piculet, a small wood-pecker, on the wrong side of the path, they immediately came to a halt. Sometimes they insisted on abandoning the task in hand and returning to camp; on other occasions they sat around waiting for a more auspicious sign to encourage them to continue. This respect for birds was not limited to flesh-and-blood creatures. Birds appearing in dreams also could interfere with our plans. After one such visitation Bahat postponed a trip downriver that we had all been looking forward to.

In time my own attitudes to birds became deeply coloured by Dusun and Iban beliefs. Indeed, I found myself seeing birdlife through native eyes. During my solitary trips away from camp, when I was alone for days at a stretch, I began to appreciate the extent to which the birds' presence dominated the jungle. How dead the forest would be without the flutter of wings in the green canopy and the cheerful harmony of hoots, trills and twitters. The birds were a constant source of delight to me—good omens in a sense. How could I be sad, angry or even lonely when surrounded by such gaiety and life?

There are nearly 600 species of bird in Borneo. They are adapted to every type of habitat and every part of the forest: sea birds round the coast, riverine birds along the twisted waterways, and in the jungle, the greatest variety of all. Some, like the fast-running pheasants and multi-coloured pittas, live on the forest floor feeding on insects and fallen fruit; others like the bright green barbets and restless flycatchers inhabit the middle storey, while the pigeons and hornbills are at home in the high canopy, searching among the fruiting trees for food. Each species has its own distinctive habits, its own characteristic diet, its own song, its own special niche. At any time of day or night different birds will be active in different places; woodpeckers foraging around tree trunks in broad daylight, owls and frogmouths hunting in the dark.

One of the birds I saw most frequently was the Brahminy kite, the commonest bird of prey in Borneo and a good illustration of the complexity of Bornean views on birds. A pair of these neat brown, white and black scavengers nested near our camp and wheeled around us whenever we gutted pigs or fish, swooping boldly to snatch choice pieces of offal. To my Dusun helpers the Brahminy kite was just a pest, vermin to be pelted with stones. But the Kenyah tribes, for example, regard the same Brahminy kite as the most important omen bird, while the Ibans believe it is the earthly form of Singalang Burong, the highest god of war. Although in his behaviour as a bird Singalang Burong reveals no messages himself, he can convey warnings to the Ibans through one or more of his sons-in-law, each in their own feathered guise as trogons, woodpeckers shamas and others. To complicate matters further, the ritual of bird augury is never static. New fashions evolve in the scattered long-houses, and gradually gain popularity throughout a tribe.

Among the Ibans, for example, the Brahminy kite is a usurper, having ousted a much finer bird from its former status as supreme avian god.

This dethroned deity is the rhinoceros hornbill. It is not hard to see why it should have caught the imagination of Bornean natives. It is a spectacular bird, three and a half feet long, and is named after the up-curved red horn or casque which rises above its powerful bill. With this phallic adornment and its jocular, raucous behaviour, the rhinoceros hornbill epitomized masculine virility to the head-hunting Dyaks. The cock bird's habit of imprisoning his mate in a dark hole at breeding time no doubt also appealed to the warriors' ideas of male dominance. Ibans made stylized wooden carvings of rhinoceros horn-bills, exaggerating the horn into a sweeping spiral festooned with deco-rative figures and embellishments, and used them as the centre pieces of military ritual. Before a head-hunting raid, they held a ceremony to "vitalize" these totems and send their spirits on ahead to attack the enemy. The carvings are still sacred and used in religious festivals, but the living rhinoceros hornbill has declined in spiritual significance to such an extent that it is now regarded as little more than food.

One of these birds makes a good meal for a large family and hornbill hunters are skilled in catching them, either when the birds are nesting or by imitating the adult's harsh croak and so luring the prey within shooting distance. I had great success with the trick myself, using a tape recorder. Hidden in a bush I broadcast recorded hornbill calls and soon attracted two of these gargantuan birds. They arrived, flapping heavily from tree to tree, and peered suspiciously down, their startling red eyes combing the undergrowth for some sign of the unseen challenger as they replied angrily to every burst from the tape recorder.

Later, I discovered that in a hole in a huge tree at the top of a ridge behind my camp, a pair of rhinoceros hornbills were nesting. Unfor-tunately I missed the walling up of the female. It is a fascinating rite: when a hen hornbill is ready to lay, she enters the nest hole and begins to seal the entrance from inside using her sticky droppings as cement. Meanwhile the male may also build from the outside, using mud. When the work is finished, the female bird is incarcerated by a solid wall in which only a narrow slit remains, just big enough for her to put her beak through to receive food and to dispose of her droppings. This wall is presumably an effective defence against snakes, civets and monkeys that might otherwise raid the nest.

I often saw the male taking fruit and large crickets to his mate. He never returned direct to her nest but broke his journey at a nearby perch

Panting in the tropical heat, a female rhinoceros hornbill flaunts the horny, upcurved projection, or casque, that gives the species its name. Although this hollow ornament is possessed by both sexes, it is much larger in the male, which suggests that it has some part to play in courtship and territorial displays.

#

where he could scan the forest and ensure that all was safe. Once satisfied, he flew direct to the hole and passed his offerings to his imprisoned partner, whose beak I could see protruding from the slit.

This is a dangerous time for the female if Bornean natives are out hunting. Locating the nest by the tell-tale pile of droppings on the forest floor, the determined collector will scale a great tree, pegging flimsy sapling ladders together to reach the prized cache. He hacks open the entrance, lifts out any fat chicks that have hatched and twists a thorny twig round in the cavity until he has speared the unfortunate hen.

I wanted no such fate to befall this family, so I told no one at camp about my discovery, and visited the nest only occasionally to see whether the female and young had chipped themselves out. Among hornbills, this is usually quite a protracted procedure. When the female lays an egg, she begins incubating immediately: she has no option, being penned up in such a small space. If she lays more than one egg, each may hatch at a different time, and the chicks will be ready to leave the nest on different dates. But the first bird to depart is the mother, keen to escape the increasingly crowded family home. After she has chipped her way out, the young wall themselves up again, and the process is repeated until the last chick has gone. I made the mistake of neglecting my find for a few days, and when I returned, the entrance was open and the hole was empty. From time to time I found a young rhinoceros hornbill in the vicinity, a fine bird with a clear blue iris. I like to think it came from the nest I had seen and that by keeping my secret I was in some way responsible for its safety.

The casques of hornbills are usually hollow. But one Bornean species, the helmeted hornbill, has a solid casque which has become much prized over the centuries as a material for carving. During the Ming Dynasty hornbill ivory was valued by Chinese traders at twice the price of elephant ivory, and skilled craftsmen exercised their art in carving decorative belt buckles, ornamental statuettes and snuff bottles from it.

For me the helmeted hornbill is most memorable for its intricate call, which is one of the unique sounds of the Bornean jungle. The full call is a prolonged affair performed by the male. The song begins with a series of clear hoots—*took, took*—at five second intervals. Gradually the call speeds up with successive hoots coming faster and faster at increasing pitch until they explode into a climax of whooping chuckles that slowly die down to a mocking cackle of maniacal laughter. The whole call is aptly summed up by a Malay nickname for the helmeted hornbill, the *burong tebang mentua* or chop-down-your-mother-in-law bird. This derives from a fable according to which the preliminary *tooks* signify the sound of a young man's axe as he chops the stilts of the house where his domineering mother-in-law lies sleeping. As the supports begin to give way he strikes faster and faster, and the bird's cackling finale beautifully expresses the youth's evil glee as the house crashes down.

A week after Bahat had postponed one of our trips downriver, on account of the inauspicious birds in his dreams, we began to run short of rice and it became imperative that we should go down to his *kampong* for new supplies. This time the omens were auspicious, and we set out on a trip that taught me some new complexities in the local attitudes to birds. Some birds elicited not a trace of superstition. Bahat's children, armed with catapults, were often out scouring the woods and river-banks in search of pets. On finding a suitable bird, they fired their catapults; capturing their stunned prey, they tied a piece of string to its leg, tethered it to their clothing and carried it with them wherever they went. Some birds became quite tame, but many died.

Bahat was equally undeterred by superstition in combatting the birds that threatened the crops of hill rice he had planted outside the *kampong*. He erected small bamboo huts in the rice field; from these he strung an intricate web of strings, leading above the green shoots to bamboo clappers on poles. By pulling on a string, a lookout inside one of the huts could raise a piece of bamboo and drop it again to make a sharp report that put the feeding flocks to flight. Raised bridges linked the huts and shouting children would run from one to another, operating the bird-scarers in all parts of the field.

While Bahat showed me these painstaking preparations, he told me of the rather different role played by birds in agriculture in the Kelabit highlands. Because of Borneo's constant equatorial climate, there are of course no conventional seasons to guide the farmer; but the tropics provide a winter refuge for many bird migrants that spend the summer breeding in the temperate hinterland of Asia, and the regular comings and goings of these visitors tell the Kelabit people when to plant their crops. Different months of the Kelabit calendar are named after the various migrants. When the yellow wagtail is seen on the open upland clearings in August, the villagers know it is time to clear the rice fields for planting. By October the brown shrike has arrived and the farmers must hurry to finish their sowing.

My biggest surprise in the *kampong* was the discovery that Dusun bird superstitions extend to the common domestic fowl. There were plenty of chickens in the village, and Bahat intended to take some back with us to the Segama camp. I fondly imagined that we would enjoy regular eggs and an occasional pullet to break the monotony of our normal diet of fish and wild pig meat. But I soon discovered that in the *kampong* chickens were only killed on special occasions and the eating of eggs was almost taboo. I later learned that the original domestication of the chicken from the red jungle fowl (still widespread over much of tropical Asia though absent from Borneo) was probably not for food but for religious reasons: to frighten away evil spirits in the forest, and for divinations and sacrifices at festivals.

The eggs have a special significance for Dusuns. Many believe that the first people hatched from a giant bird's egg. Eagles' eggs are regarded as powerful magic and a chicken's egg is sufficiently potent for use at cleansing ceremonies to remove evil spirits that cause sickness and pain. Village magicians believe they can cure a migraine by rolling eggs over the suffering man's body and by sucking at his skin, while gongs drum incessantly and blindfolded men dance to provide the right atmosphere.

Bahat clearly intended his chickens to serve some other purpose than mere eating, and I never did find out what that purpose was. When we returned to our camp, the fowls laid and bred prolifically. Nobody took much trouble to protect the chicks from snakes, hawks or monitor lizards, but in all my time in the forest we never ate eggs or chickens.

This regard for chickens seemed all the more extraordinary when compared with the natives' willingness to eat the once-revered rhinoceros hornbill and even the magnificent Argus pheasant, which is widely accorded a ceremonial importance. The Argus pheasant is perhaps the finest bird of the Bornean rain forest. The cock has superb wing coverts, long broad feathers marked with rows of delicately shaded "eyes" that spread out to form a fan like a peacock's tail. The wing feathers are kept by Dyak warriors as trophies to be worn on ceremonial costumes at feasts and dances. The Argus pheasant motif is also commonly used by the Ibans in tattoos—an appropriate choice, for according to a native legend the bird gained its own elegant markings by tattoo at the hands of the dowdy coucal, a member of the cuckoo family. The pheasant and the coucal had agreed to decorate each other so as to disguise themselves against their enemies. The skilful coucal spent hours painting the pheasant's beautiful eye markings; but the Argus pheasant, being a lazy creature, could not be bothered to carry out his side of the agreement. As he was about to begin, he cried out that danger was approaching, poured the pots of plain pigment over the coucal and

The male crested green wood partridge, a relative of the exotic great Argus pheasant, is festooned with all the eye-catching qualities so vital to the courtship activities of birds that live on the shaded forest floor. The magnificent plume, the red of the bill and the intricately frilled skin around the eye help the suitor to lure females.

ran off, leaving the bird with a plain blue body and rust coloured wings.

Often while I was in the forest I heard the Argus pheasant calling. Typically the cock calls several times each morning, emitting a clear double note up to a dozen times, which earns the bird its onomatopoeic Dusun name of *tuboh*. Every cock has its own "dancing" ring, a roughly circular area of level ground about 20 feet across, which he keeps cleared of leaves and seedlings. Here he spends his mornings, tidying the arena or performing to attract a mate. He can afford to be unconcerned about the dangers of predatory cats and civets, for he has prepared several escape tunnels through the vegetation, and he is endowed with such acute eyesight and hearing that at the first hint of danger he can be away.

Many natives who have hunted in the forest all their lives have never seen the cock on his dancing ring. Dozens of times when I heard one calling I crept up stealthily only to find that he had vanished and I had been thwarted again. It was quite by chance that I finally came across a ring at the top of a small hill where a dense mass of rattan vines formed a convenient screen behind which I could hide to watch the incumbent. Even so, I usually caught little more than a glimpse of his long grey body sneaking away. A few times I was rewarded by seeing the bird give his territorial cry, *tuboh*, *tuboh*, dipping his naked blue head twice in a curious bob as he called. These rare occasions were exciting enough, but once I had the great fortune of surprising him unawares and was able to watch the entire courtship display of this incredible pheasant.

It was my birthday but I had nothing and no one to celebrate with, so I headed off into the forest along one of my well used trails. As I drew near the Argus pheasant's ring, I heard an unusual rustling ahead. Under cover of the noise I crept forwards and ducked quickly behind the accommodating buttress of a vast tree. As I peered cautiously round the trunk I saw the male bird strutting about his ring, long tail held high and head bobbing low to the ground. Suddenly the cock fanned out his amazing spread of eye-bedecked wing coverts to form a complete screen in front of his body. It was a breathtaking sight. He held this position for only a few moments then lowered his fans very slowly, shaking the feathers to produce the curious rattling sound that had first attracted my attention. I could not see the hen for whose benefit this display was made, but I decided that she must be concealed in the undergrowth outside the dancing ring. Once more the cock fanned his plumes to perform his bizarre dance, then abruptly he abandoned his courtship. What disturbed him I never knew, but he obviously sensed something was wrong and scuttled quietly away through the jungle brush.

The hen pheasant is so different from the cock in size, colour and behaviour that the Dusuns ascribe to her a quite different name: *Kawau*. It is she, they say, who is responsible for the repeated *wau, wau, wau* call that can be heard in the forest at any time of day or night. Several learned ornithologists believe, however, that this call is not made by the hen but by the cocks while they are wandering away from their rings. The secretive habits of the Argus pheasant will no doubt guarantee that it is a long time before the mystery is finally solved.

I saw and heard many other fascinating birds in the Bornean forests: gorgeous sunbirds, gay broadbills, emerald leafbirds, whistling mynahs, gaudy parrots and tropical kingfishers whose brilliant blue plumes were once popular with Chinese courtiers for fashioning into jewellery. I spent happy hours watching tiny green and scarlet lorikeets feeding daintily on the flowers of the tallest trees. These pretty birds are nicknamed hanging parrots from their habit of sleeping in neat rows in communal roosts, hanging upside down from the branches. But of all the fantastic birds of the Bornean jungle, I would single out one of the drabbest and commonest species, the yellow-crowned bulbul, as that which gave me the most pleasure. A bold cock lived close to the camp. Day after day he sat in his bush, singing his heart out when the rest of the forest was quiet. His magnificent solo of rich warbled notes could compare with any other bird song in the world. The yellow-crowned bulbul has to sing well, for according to native bird-lore, he sings for his life. He owed a longstanding debt to the crocodile but could not afford to pay it back. Instead he borrowed the loud song of the chestnut-collared kingfisher and went down to the river to soothe his creditor. Later when the kingfisher asked for his call back, the bulbul refused. The kingfisher retaliated by swearing an oath that the yellow-crowned bulbul should never return to the jungle where all the other bulbuls belonged. So now the bird lives only by the river, still singing to the crocodile.

6/ Mangroves and Monkeys

*From the obstacle that these roots and the mud present, a
mangrove swamp is one of the most difficult and
fatiguing things in the world to traverse. To live in it would
be the most abominable of existences, if only for the
myriads of mosquitoes that swarm in it.*

ODOARDO BECCARI/ WANDERINGS IN THE GREAT FORESTS OF BORNEO

The outline of Borneo is constantly changing. In some places the sea
nibbles away at the land, gradually eroding sandstone cliffs. But mostly
the island is expanding, spreading out into the shallow coastal waters.
Where the breaking waves cast up soft white sand, the beaches are stab-
ilized by wiry grasses, feathery Casuarina trees and spiny-leaved pan-
dans. Along the sheltered coasts, the rivers pour out their cargoes of silt
and build up a basement of mud between the land and the out-growing
coral reefs. On this slimy foothold grow nipah palms and the land-
building mangrove trees, forming the evergreen belt fringing the sea.

Salt water swirls in around the mangroves' trunks twice a day, yet
the trees actually prosper in these inhospitable conditions. The pioneer-
ing species at the low tide mark constantly push forward their lateral
roots, and behind them come the mangroves of the second and third
ranks, consolidating the work with arching, stilt-like roots and woody
knees that loop in and out of the mud. Advancing together, the three main
zones of mangroves tenaciously reclaim the sea, extending their own
environment at a startling pace. In northern Sarawak, the Baram and
Limbang flood plains grow no less than 90 feet a year, and towns built
on the coast are soon left several miles inland.

The mangrove swamp is a world of green and grey, of slimy mud,
soupy water and tangled roots. Initially the effect is ugly and forbidding.
The heat is extreme and the smell from stagnant ooze unpleasant. Pas-

sage is difficult, for the clinging mud drags at your boots, and clouds of mosquitoes and fierce biting ants provide constant persecution. To these inconveniences are added the hazards of entangled rootlets, spiky seedlings dropped by the intermingling nipah palms, and sharp-edged shells. There are also dangerous sea snakes and 25-foot crocodiles.

The mangroves have an irresistible magnetism for the naturalist. Both terrestrial and marine creatures live in this no-man's land at the edge of the sea. Consequently, more classes of the animal kingdom are found here than in any other habitat. Fish that walk and others that shoot down insects with jets of water, ants that weave with silk, and gregarious fireflies that turn whole trees into glowing beacons with the coming of night—these are some of the unique lures.

Borneo's mangrove swamps are similar to others found in the Old World and New World tropics, but they have an extra richness. They are several miles wide in places, and contain the greatest number of mangrove tree species: around 30 in all. Above all, they are the only place in the world where you can see the extraordinary, long-nosed proboscis monkeys, a species that feeds on the leaves of the *Sonneratia* tree. Malays refer to these colourful, amusing creatures as *kera belanda* or "Dutchmen monkeys" because their long red noses look like those of sunburnt Europeans. *Kera belanda* are quite unlike other monkeys and little is known of their habits.

I had heard that proboscis monkeys were often seen in the mangroves about three miles along the coast from Lahad Datu, the town to which I came when I needed to buy more supplies for my Segama camp. On one such journey from the interior, I made a special visit to this spot, approaching the mangrove fringe from inland. Full of enthusiasm, I set off along a winding path, and soon ventured off into the dank, fetid tangle on one side. Slowly I squelched towards the sea, grabbing at flimsy saplings for support as I picked my way across the maze of roots. A black and yellow banded snake lay coiled in the branches of a low bush. It was almost certainly one of the harmless mangrove snakes, but I wasn't going to look any closer, as the poisonous kraits are almost identically patterned.

After a couple of hours I was tired, sticky and sore, and thankful to return to the footpath. I had not seen any monkeys but the visit had been made memorable by the abundance of two other inhabitants of the swamp: the clouds of mosquitoes that followed me wherever I went and the menacing weaver ants that rushed towards me whenever I brushed against their nest trees. These large, rusty red ants build their dangling

Continued on page 122

ANTS SWARMING OUT TO REPAIR THE NEST

DRAWING THE LEAF EDGES TOGETHER

A LARVA (CENTRE) BEING USED AS A SHUTTLE

Ants that Weave Castles in the Air

Weaver ants have adapted with stunning ingenuity to an arboreal life-style, living in leaf nests that dangle among the branches and hang from six to 20 feet above ground. The nests are rather untidy structures, envelopes of five or six leaves held together with thick webs of silk filament. The worker ants obtain this material from their own larvae which are equipped with silk-spinning glands.

When the nest is torn apart—by a violent storm or, as in this case, by a curious naturalist—the worker ants swarm outside on full alert and immediately begin repair operations. They bridge the large gaps by forming themselves into a tangled, living chain and draw the leaves together. Simultaneously, another corps of workers brings up the white larvae from the inside of the nest, ready to start what can almost be described as weaving.

With the leaves in position, the ants squeeze the larvae to make them secrete their sticky strands (one of them can be seen in the jaws of the ant in the middle of the bottom left picture). The ants then pass these living shuttles to and fro across the joined leaves.

The seam is finally closed by a combined enterprise: a few ants stand on one side of the rend and tug the further leaf edge into alignment, while others complete the woven join on the inside of the nest.

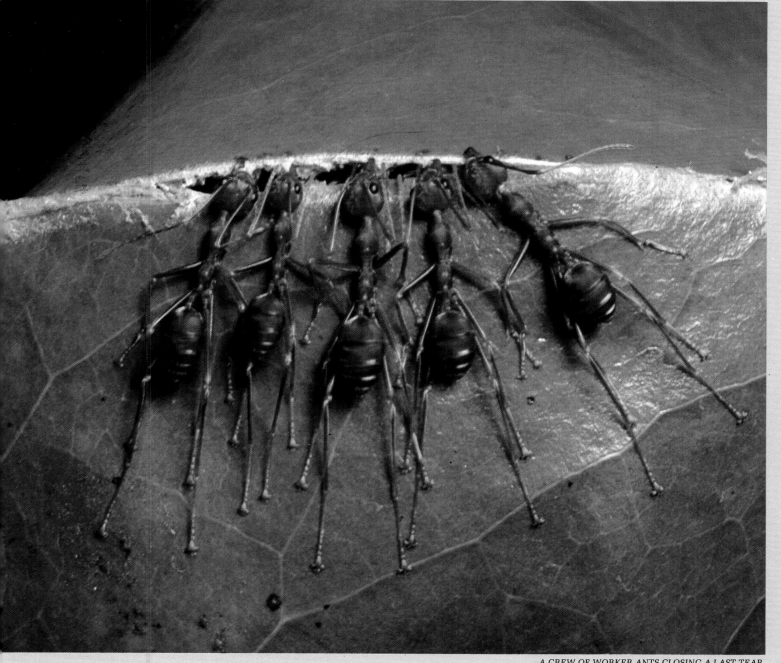

A CREW OF WORKER ANTS CLOSING A LAST TEAR

nests by weaving leaves together with fine silk threads. Dozens of workers stream in and out of their homes, and the two-way traffic extends along the branches, down the trunks and on to the muddy ground. Flies, grasshoppers, crickets, and anything small that moves, are seized and dragged back to the nest where the large queen is busy laying more eggs. Unlike the worker ants, the queen is green, perhaps because any predator that broke into the nest would not notice her against the background of leaves, but would concentrate on attacking the red workers. Even if only a dozen ants survived with the queen, the future of the colony would be secure.

Curious to see what would happen, I tore a gap in one of the leaf nests that was hanging only a few feet above me. Immediately hundreds of angry red ants dashed out and swarmed furiously over their devastated home, inspecting the damage. Repair work was soon in progress. One ant stood on the lower edge and, reaching up, seized the leaf above with its jaws and drew the two together. Soon another had joined in, then another and another, until after a few minutes there was a neat row of figures clamping the two sides of the rend firmly together. I could just discern other ants inside the nest moving back and forth across the gap, mending the tear with their silk strands. The weavers were not secreting the silk themselves but were carrying ant larvae in their jaws, and it was these grubs that produced the sticky thread. As the larvae were passed backwards and forwards like spindles on a loom, the leaves were bound together until there was no trace of the damage left.

By the time I was making my way back towards Lahad Datu, the tide was out and the exposed mudflats were a scene of busy activity. I hastened to investigate, stepping carefully across the drying mud. There was no shade from the cruel sun and the light reflecting from the wet patches was dazzling. Crabs scuttled to and fro and mudskippers skittered over the slippery surface, searching for tiny crustaceans.

Mudskippers are exceptional fish for they can leave the water and move freely on land. A fish out of water has two main difficulties: obtaining oxygen with gills designed for underwater use, and moving around without legs. Mudskippers have solved both problems. They breathe by carrying a mixture of water and air in their gill chambers; this keeps their gills moist and serves as a filter for incoming oxygen. Every time they feed, however, they lose vital water and have to rush to the nearest puddle to replenish their supply. To facilitate travel on land, mud-skippers have specially adapted pectoral fins on which they can lever themselves forward, and with a lash from their stiffened tails they can dart across either mud or water. Their pelvic fins are perhaps even more useful. They are fused to form a sucker which enables the mudskipper to climb and cling to tree roots and trunks. No mean achievement for a fish!

These are not the mudskippers' only adaptations for an amphibious life. Their eyes are situated high on the head so that they give a good view on land or protrude above the surface of the water when the rest of the fish is submerged. These goggling protuberances make the little torpedo-shaped mudskippers look strange enough, but the eye surfaces have to be kept moist, and the method employed for this purpose makes the fish odder still. Several mudskippers near me were blinking constantly as though in a state of nervous surprise. In fact they were merely rolling their eyes, wetting them in pools of water inside the sockets.

Some of the male mudskippers had excavated little watery craters in the mud: nests in which females would lay eggs—provided that the males could attract mates and then keep their rivals at bay. These problems gave rise to some of the strangest sights on the mudflats. One mudskipper was attempting to catch the eye of a potential mate by flipping himself sideways and jumping several inches vertically upwards, erecting two colourful dorsal fins like flags. I saw another fish performing a less strenuous display to warn off other males, simply slithering about on the mud and erecting his foremost fin from time to time. Near the low tide mark opposing males of a larger type of mudskipper were settling their differences more emphatically. Two antagonists turned to face each other and suddenly lunged forwards with mouths agape and fins raised. The duo lurched back and forth for a few moments, then advanced and locked their wide mouths. They pushed mightily for a few seconds until one lost ground and backed away.

Mingling freely among the mudskippers were enormous numbers of colourful little crabs and big, conical snails that ploughed slowly through the mud. Stalk-eyed crabs were busy feeding, squabbling and courting before the next tide came sweeping in to send them scrambling for the refuge of their dark burrows. Most were fiddler crabs, and the males of this group could easily be recognised by the prominent great claw borne on one arm. In some cases the right claw was so enlarged and in others the left: it did not seem to matter which.

The function of this huge appendage soon becomes obvious to even the casual observer. Males spend a lot of time guarding their territory and threatening one another, waving their giant claws menacingly at any intruder who dares to come too close to their burrow entrances. At the same time the male is constantly on the lookout for a female, and, should one take his fancy, the suitor beckons in comically exaggerated fashion with his huge pincer. Most of the females I saw, however, seemed more interested in feeding. Their tiny feet moved speedily up and down like the drummings of a wild pianist as they gathered tiny scraps of algae and plankton from the thin film left by the receding tide.

The fiddler crabs were cavorting in their hundreds only a few yards in front of me, but when I stepped forward to get a closer look at them they darted for the safety of their burrows. So I tried a new tactic, crouching down and remaining absolutely still. After a minute or two the first crabs cautiously emerged, raising first one and then the other stalked eye. Soon normal activity was resumed and I found myself surrounded by the tiny dramas of everyday crab life. A small male being chased by a larger rival, disappeared down the nearest burrow. Unfortunately the rightful owner was in residence. Within seconds the fugitive was fiercely ejected back into the path of his antagonist, and the chase continued. Two other males locked claws in a trial of strength, turning and twisting from side to side, straining to break the deadlock. A pretty blue and orange crab weaved an arrogant trail through the ranks of the pink and white commoners, and one unfortunate that had lost three legs worked with frantic speed to clear his burrow of mud before he was swamped by the incoming sea.

There was one creature I did not see on this occasion, and that was the rare king crab. In fact, it is not a crab but a relative of the extinct sea scorpions. The king crab is truly a living fossil. Its large horseshoe-shaped carapace, some two feet across, protects a harmless organism with ten feeble limbs, and in this form the creature has remained almost unchanged through 400 million years. King crabs spend most of their lives in the sea, but they return to the intertidal mudflats to breed. The female excavates a shallow depression to house her two or three thousand eggs, while the male clambers in ungainly fashion on to her back to fertilize the eggs as they are deposited.

After my failure to find proboscis monkeys on my first trip, I decided that perhaps my best plan was to approach the mangrove swamps from the sea. I borrowed a Forest Department launch and engaged a boatman to accompany me. It was a gorgeous, clear day and the sea was happily calm as we set out. The outboard motor purred easily and we headed south, keeping parallel to the green coastline. The sea bottom changed suddenly from silty-brown to bluey-white and we were above a coral reef, the outermost stage in the reclamation of the land from the sea.

The asparagus-shaped roots of the Sonneratia tree protrude above mud and salt water at low tide in a mangrove swamp. The roots absorb oxygen through tiny pores in their surface, and transfer the oxygen to other roots lying beneath the mud. Without the benefit of these air-breathing roots, the mangrove tree would suffocate.

Warm shallow waters like these are ideal for the growth of coral polyps, tiny animals that leave behind calcium skeletons when they die and gradually build the reef upwards and outwards, generation upon generation. The corals act as a barrier to trap the mud pouring out from the mouths of the rivers, and so prepare the way for the mangroves' advance.

We stopped the engine and drifted idly for a while above this solid band of white splashed with red, black and yellow. Through the clear water I could see the beautiful patterns of smooth-mazed brain corals, sharp-edged lettuce corals and delicately branching staghorns. Blue parrot fish, yellow butterfly fish, spiny sea urchins, waving anemonies and striped sea snakes went about their silent business beneath us.

I was roused from my reverie by a loud splash to seawards, probably caused, my companion advised, by one of the huge, flat, flapping manta rays which inhabit these waters, together with mackerel and sharks. The tide was now high and we headed towards the coastline, floating right in under the dense, layered wall of mangroves, which were mantled right down to the high water mark with shiny green leaves rustling in the light sea breeze.

Here we were looking at the pioneer trees, the most seaward of the three main types of mangroves, and before the trip ended we had an excellent view of the two more landward zones as well. While we continued our search for the proboscis monkeys, we were able to see not only the methods by which the different mangroves breathe when their roots are submerged, but also how they manage to reproduce in this harsh environment.

The front line of mangroves is dominated by the intrepid *Sonneratia* and *Avicennia* species, which take hold just above the level of the lowest tides. As they advance out to sea, following some distance behind the coral reefs, they stabilize the mud with their roots, binding the fine silt particles and trapping debris brought in on the tides. Because their roots are almost constantly submerged by suffocating mud and sea water, these trees have evolved their own peculiar breathing system. They send up thousands of thin vertical rootlets which reach above the mud and water to breathe for the large roots below, so creating the impression of a flooded asparagus bed.

Other types of plant have aerial roots, but the mangroves are special in that they possess a whole range of adaptations for coping with their wet and salty environment. Unlike most plants they have developed ways of desalinating water, so that the sap inside the tree is less salty than the water surrounding the roots. The leaves have special glands to excrete what salt they do absorb. Most ingenious of all is their fruiting behaviour. Many mangroves flower all the time, often when the tree has reached only sapling stage. Some are also unusual in their seeding, for the first root and leaf germinate while the fruit is still on the tree.

This remarkable feat is the speciality of the Rhizophora trees which colonize the higher mud banks and form the second rank in the mangrove advance, the zone submerged only by high tides. As we steered up a narrow creek behind the pioneer fringe, we found ourselves among the Rhizophora trees, and I soon saw several large seedlings hanging from the branches: brown, globular knobs containing the future leaves. Already they had roots growing down beneath them: glistening, green drop spears as thick as a man's thumb and up to two feet long. As soon as the young plant can survive on its own, it drops off the branch. The long green spear enters the water with scarcely a ripple and lodges in the soft mud below. More roots grow from the lower end of the spear, a shoot appears from the top of the knob, and a new mangrove tree is quickly on its way.

In maturity a Rhizophora possesses the stilt-like roots which are so characteristic a feature of mangrove swamps, forming an almost impenetrable barrier. The roots radiate from the main trunk, arching outwards and then plunging down into the mud. In this way they act as supports for the tree in the shifting mud, and they are liberally supplied with lenticels, or air pores, which allow oxygen down to the lower roots.

We put up the outboard motor and rowed farther up the creek. Large snails, disturbed by the wash, heaved themselves laboriously up the maze of roots beside us. Mudskippers slithered down to plop into the water, and long-nosed garfish shoaled back and forth beneath our bows. My attention was caught by a spray of water droplets that rose vertically from beneath one of the mangrove bushes, splashing on to the leaves of a low branch. As we drew nearer the spot, I could see the creature responsible for this, a stubby, leaf-shaped fish marked with bold black bars. It was one of the well-named archer fish. The marksman rose to the surface again and squirted a powerful jet of water some five feet into the air. A small caterpillar was dislodged from the branch by the spray and fell into the water where it was quickly gobbled up by the fish.

By now we were near the high tide mark and the Rhizophora were giving way to the buttressed Bruguiera trees of the third mangrove zone. Bruguiera send out distinctive looping roots that curl away; now below, now above ground. The roots fulfil a respiratory function like those of *Rhizophoras*, but they are rarely submerged by the sea. Scattered among the *Bruguieras* and lining the sides of the creek were a few of the elegant nipah palms that dominate the estuarine regions of Borneo. Between the *Bruguiera* zone and the true rain forest on higher ground there is usually a band of damp, swampy peat forest. I wanted to continue further up our small creek to investigate this, but the boatman was keen to return because the tide was dropping, and if we delayed any longer we would be trapped in the mud until the night flood tide.

We turned back towards the sea and headed for Lahad Datu. Suddenly, among the trees by the water's edge, we saw a group of large red-nosed monkeys. They were *kera belanda*, the proboscis or Dutchman monkeys. Unfortunately the mud prevented us from coming in close to shore and we had to be content with only a brief glimpse before they crashed heavily away, deeper into the swamp and out of sight.

On subsequent occasions I had a little more luck in my search for the proboscis monkeys. Several times on the lower reaches of the Segama river I managed to manoeuvre quite close to them. So long as I kept my boat moving they paid scant attention to me, but whenever I tried to land the whole troop would take flight, leaping and crashing through the tree-tops. On one such sighting a male monkey jumped clean into the river near me. I do not know whether this was by accident or design, but he took advantage of my surprise and swam underwater for a considerable distance before surfacing well away from me. As the troop made its getaway, the big males brought up the rear, uttering curious honking barks to warn off any pursuers. It is when they are honking like this that the unique "sunburnt Dutchmen" look most comical. The male's long, pendulous, red nose, bizarre enough at the best of times, shoots up into the most ludicrous horizontal position with each warning bark. I found it extremely hard to take such a comical threat seriously, but presumably other animals are warned to keep their distance.

The shyness of these strange monkeys and the extreme difficulty of following them through their swampy haunts made me despair of ever getting close to them. But eventually I got my chance on the south coast of Kalimantan. Surprisingly, it was close to the thriving metropolis of Bandjarmasin at Pulau Kembang, an island about half a mile long and only about two hundred yards wide, in the middle of the swirling Barito river. A boy agreed to take me out in his boat, assuring me as we chugged slowly out through a patch of floating water hyacinths that the big monkeys with red noses did live there. Huge cargo ships passed up and down the river, and laden *prahu* bobbed across the choppy water. It seemed incredible that proboscis monkeys could exist beside so much human activity, but in Borneo the wilderness encroaches closely upon the towns and villages. Certainly Pulau Kembang offered ample evidence of wildlife. We passed a tree full of bee-eaters, their multi-coloured plumage providing a splash of brilliant colour, and groups of crab-eating macaques scampered along the river bank, picking over the debris at the low tide mark. Two Brahminy kites perched on the stark branch of a dead tree, and high in the clear sky a fish eagle wheeled easily on the rising air currents.

As we rounded the end of the island, I spotted two big male proboscis monkeys in a small mangrove tree. When we landed they leapt away, but I was able to follow them on foot, managing to keep just a few trees behind them until a honeycomb of sunken, muddy pools barred my way, sending me despondently back to the boat.

The boat boy, however, was more optimistic, and as we chugged on along the shore his persistence was finally rewarded: we came across a whole troop of proboscis monkeys scampering along the beach to a stand of tall, grey trees. The boy insisted that we should go on and land beyond them, and in a short time we arrived at a curious narrow pier that led to a small Chinese temple inhabited by a group of tame macaque monkeys who rushed to greet us in the hope of tit-bits. The boy explained that these gregarious macaques had, by their example, encouraged the proboscis monkeys to grow accustomed to the pilgrims. Now we could see the group of bulky proboscis foraging for new shoots in the branches of some *Sonneratia* mangroves, their main source of food. Closer and closer they came, their coats shining in the clear afternoon light. A big male, acting sentinel at the top of a tree, squatted in a hunched position, peering down his long nose at us.

Here on Pulau Kembang food was in short supply, so the 20 to 30 animals that performed before us were a small group by proboscis monkey standards. Gradually they circled away, leaping agilely from one bough to the next, a female with a clinging infant making heavy landing crashes. Although the party were scattered, the party kept in contact by means of the curious deep honking of the adult males. As darkness fell they made their way across the island to their sleeping posts. I spent a delightful evening watching them settle, hurtling one by one across a wide gap to two isolated trees where they arranged themselves in orderly fashion along the branches, their thick white tails hanging neatly down. The last proboscis monkey to cross was the biggest

One of Borneo s oddities, a proboscis monkey, lounges in a Sonneratia tree from which it has stripped and eaten most of the leaves.

male, who remained on guard, eyeing me through the evening mist.

Nightfall marks a change of shifts among the creatures of the mangrove swamps, and the change-over is possibly even more dramatic than in the high rain forest. While I was in Borneo, I had several chances to watch the coastal night begin. By the time the monkeys have retired to their posts and flocks of pigeons and elegant white egrets have returned to their roosts, the great flying foxes, or fruit bats, are ready to embark on their feeding expeditions. During the day they have hung from the mangroves in great restless colonies, fanning their large wings to keep cool in the midday heat. As darkness approaches, thousands upon thousands of shrieking bats detach themselves from their communal roosts and flap away on their four-foot wingspans. In a long, meandering chain they follow the coastline and then break away inland in twos and threes to dine on sweet fruits and succulent shoots in the swampy forest.

While the fruit bats are away on their nocturnal journeys, the mangroves come alive with luminous creatures. The waters of the creeks are usually thick with phosphorescent plankton, and you can see fish darting away from the wake of a boat: shadowy phantoms making brief appearances like underwater comets. But there is another and more spectacular display in the mangroves: the flashing, pulsating light-show put on by the *Pteropteryx* fireflies. They are known locally as *kelip-kelip*, a word accurately representing the click-click precision with which these beetles flash on and off.

It was a still, close evening when I ventured out in search of the *kelip-kelip*, muffled in an anorak for protection more against mosquitoes than the cold. As I wandered down a long wooden catwalk that cut through the mangrove swamp to the sea, I could hear the splash of mudskippers disturbed by my approach and the flutter of bats hunting midges and moths. Far across the water the mournful song of a Malay fisherman contrasted with the dull burr of the frogs and crickets and the gentle rustling of the mangrove leaves. Although the sky was still pink with the setting sun, the first fireflies were already beginning to wink at the top of a small *Sonneratia* tree. As darkness grew the signal was slowly taken up by other fireflies and, branch by branch, the lights spread, uncoordinated at first but gradually becoming synchronized. Soon the whole tree seemed to be flashing on and off. Studies with recording instruments have shown that the fireflies' synchronous flashing is as regular as any biological rhythm known to exist, steadier than the heartbeat of a sleeping man.

The flashing is set up by the male fireflies to attract mates. Each species of firefly has its own distinct rhythm so that females can distinguish their kind from the rest; and different species congregate in different trees. Even then the species rhythm would be quite unrecognisable, blurred in the melee of individual lights, were it not for the fact that the insects all flashed in unison.

But why should male fireflies congregate in the first place? Why do they not wander off alone in search of a mate, as do fireflies in the rain forest? Probably the explanation is that the insects are avoiding certain dangers found in the mangrove swamps. Here there are innumerable bats which hunt on the wing and can snap up fireflies with ease. Consequently it is to the advantage of the insects to avoid flying more than they can help. They are safer stationed in a tree.

However, about half the trees in the mangrove swamps are inhabited by aggressive weaver ants, which are always ready to seize unfortunate insects that land among them. A firefly landing in a tree blindly would have a 50-50 chance of survival. But if it could tell which trees were unoccupied by ants, its chances of survival would be much greater. The first firefly to settle in a tree has no such information, but if it is able to settle and start flashing, it is an indication that ants are not present. Other fireflies may, therefore, land in safety wherever they see firefly signals, and since females are attracted too, the insects have good chances both of surviving and of finding mates. These two considerations are surely enough to attract any firefly in this hazardous environment, so more and more congregate until the tree is overflowing with *kelip-kelip*. As the same process occurs in other trees, the mangrove swamp comes alive with their wonderful illuminations.

The Walking Fish

Perhaps the most extraordinary inhabitants of Borneo's tidal mangrove swamps are the mudskippers, fish that spend much of their time out of water. Recalling the evolutionary leap perhaps 360 million years ago when aquatic creatures first came ashore, the mudskippers crawl about on the exposed mudflats at low tide. They manage this because they have adapted their breathing, ways of moving and their eyesight to land use.

The two most common species of mudskipper in Borneo are the blue-spotted *Boleophthalmus boddaerti*, which is up to seven inches long and frequents the lower parts of the mud, and the shorter, orange spotted *Periophthalmus chrysospilos*, which is happier farther inland. Both can stay submerged indefinitely, like any normal fish. But while most fish die out of water because their gills become dry, mudskippers carry a mixture of water and air in their enlarged gill chambers; and with this fishy equivalent of an aqualung they can carry a regular supply of oxygen for use on land.

To move around on firm mud, the skippers use their stubby pectoral fins like crutches and "walk". In wetter mud, they skip: they flex the tail and then with a powerful jerk, straighten it, simultaneously digging the stiffened lower edge into the mud for purchase. As if on a spring, the mudskippers leap forward as much as four feet.

Deprived of the natural wash that water provides, mudskippers keep their eyes moist by rolling them downward into a pool of liquid in the sockets. The lidless eyeball is unquestionably fish-like with its bulbous appearance, but the lens has the slightly flattened shape characteristic of land animals' eyes, for focusing on distant objects.

Mudskippers also feed on land. *Boleophthalmus* scrapes algae and minute organisms from the mud, while the smaller *Periophthalmus* goes for worms, insects, small crabs and molluscs. It is not always a graceful predator. To catch a snail, it must wait until the mollusc's body is fully extended and then rip it from the shell. An unsuccessful lunge often ends with the fish's snout buried in the mud.

When feeding, the mudskipper's stay on land is limited. Each time it opens its mouth, the gill covers relax and vital moisture gushes out with an audible burp. Within about half a minute the fish must return to water to replenish its supply.

Only the head and periscope eyes of a mudskipper show above the thick mud soup of a mangrove swamp. Unlike most fish, the mudskipper can focus on distant objects and it can spot the tiniest insect at ten feet. On sighting its quarry, the fish will often surface and pursue it ashore.

Sleek-headed Boleophthalmus line the water's edge before refilling their gill chambers with the water needed to sluice their muddy food.

A mudskipper climbs a mangrove root, hugging with its pectoral fins while its body adheres with a sucker formed by its pelvic fins.

In among the exposed mangrove roots, a small Periophthalmus sits undisturbed on the back of a Boleophthalmus. This strange habit of mudskippers has only recently been discovered, and no one knows the reason for it. The small fish has the advantage of a grandstand view, and perhaps it catches more of a breeze when raised above the mud. The Boleophthalmus gets no obvious benefit in return; it may even not have noticed it is carrying a passenger.

A *Boleophthalmus* hovers at the mouth of its burrow, used as a refuge and for breeding.

Crawling on its arm-like pectoral fins, a mudskipper can stay ashore for long periods, periodically moistening its skin in puddles.

7/ A Watery Maze

Some of the fish brought alongside were as beautiful as those celebrated in the Arabian tale, where "the fisherman, looking into the lake, saw in it fish of different colours—white, and red, and blue, and yellow".

SPENSER ST. JOHN/ *LIFE IN THE FORESTS OF THE FAR EAST*

Five hundred thousand billion gallons of rainwater deluge Borneo every year. Only a small percentage of this massive rainfall is taken up by the forest; most of it runs down to swell the complex maze of waterways. From every leaf in the jungle, droplets of water fall to form tiny downhill channels through soil and rock. Thousands of little waterfalls tinkle and bubble to feed clear streams that flow along winding boulder-strewn courses. Under the leafy roof of the tree-tops, swirling pools and chattering rivulets lead on until quite suddenly they burst out into bright daylight to join the swirling muddy brown currents of the main rivers, rushing towards the sea.

The rivers of Borneo are a biological habitat quite distinct from that of the surrounding forest. They are rich in food and minerals washed down from the woodlands, and support a wealth of life: prawns, soft-shelled turtles and fish of all shapes and sizes. Large sawfish and predatory catfish lord it over the eels, boxfish and multitudes of smaller fry that share this murky world. The wealth of fish in turn provides a living for the fish-eating birds, otters and crocodiles, while enormous monitor lizards can be seen scavenging and hunting for meat both in the water and along the river banks.

The rich riverside herbage, which flourishes in the bright sunlight, provides a better living for many large animals than does the dark forest. As evening falls and the grasshoppers fly up into the shelter of the trees, much of Borneo's big game comes out of its hiding place in the jungle to feed and drink at the bank. Shy sambur deer and the stout tembadau or wild cattle crop the grasses and ferns, while bearded pigs root for earthworms. Heavy elephants tear up *Caryota* palms, chew on wild ginger roots or crunch noisily through the thickets of bamboo.

The riverside world is also attractive to the Dusuns and Dyaks, for it is much more of a home than the gloomy jungle. The Segama river certainly played a very important part in the life of my Dusun helpers and I. It provided our drinking, cooking and washing water. It was our only line of communication with the rest of the world, and it gave us an abundant supply of fish and other river foods. Moreover, it allowed me to wander through the forest in complete confidence that I could never get lost. Whatever leaf-covered waterway I followed downstream eventually brought me back to the Segama and to camp.

Since I did not need men to help me with my work in the forest, my boatman, Bahat, and his assistant, Pingas, could spend most of their time fishing. This was no difficult task, for the Segama positively teemed with fish. The results of their efforts were usually bubbling in the pot by the time I returned to camp each evening, but on several occasions I joined in the fishing expeditions and got to know the various types at first hand. Probably all the rivers in Borneo were once as well stocked as the Segama, but over-fishing in most down-river areas prevents the fish populations from breeding to their full potential. Even 20 miles down river in Bahat's *kampong*, fish were harder to catch. We, on the other hand, were competing only against predatory animals.

A succulent species of fig commonly grew beside the river, and one particularly fruitful tree overhung the bank directly opposite our camp. This *tangkol* tree was remarkable for the number of sweet, soft, red figs it produced, and also for the number of times it came into fruit. No sooner had one harvest been eaten by hornbills and monkeys, or dropped into the swirling waters beneath, than the tree began to fruit again. Every six weeks it was laden with figs, and all the other *tangkol* trees kept in rhythm. Several types of fish capitalized on this source of food and would wait beneath the figs to gobble them as they dropped. One species in particular, the *ikan luot*, a two- to four-pound catfish, made this food its speciality. When the figs were in fruit, the *ikan luot* were plump and their meat was fatty. When the fruit was finished they became trimmer, and remained so for the few weeks until the *tangkol* fruits became available once more.

Catching *ikan luot* was child's play. No hook baited with fig, whether tossed from a boat or suspended from an overhanging branch, would be left untouched for very long. Bahat re-baited his lines each morning and evening and usually had a couple of fat *luot* for his pains. Sometimes he tried a different technique. He carved cork-shaped wooden floats, attached a short line and a baited hook to each one, then he paddled far upriver. There he tipped the lot into the water and drifted down with his lures. He collected his catch from any of the floats that were suddenly dragged violently about by a struggling victim. *Ikan luot* have to be handled with care for they carry three long poisonous spines, one on the back and one on each "shoulder". Bahat cut off these potential dangers with a *parang* as soon as he caught the fish.

The Dusuns favour *ikan luot* because of its scaleless fatty skin, rich oily meat and comparative lack of tiresome small bones. *Luot* can be simply boiled, but members of the carp family, known as *ikan tulang*, or bony fish, have to be fried crisp or charred over the camp fire. Bahat caught many *ikan tulang* by mistake while seeking *luot*. He deliberately tried for these less desirable fish only when the Segama flooded and he was forced to fish with a throw net in the mouths of small tributaries.

One fish that Bahat regarded as something of a delicacy in spite of its bony anatomy was a rarity. Anyone who has kept a tank of tropical fish is probably familiar with gouramis. Usually they are small fish with two long streamers formed by the pelvic fins. The gourami in question had trailers, too, but the creature was of enormous proportions, nearly two feet long. The fish was thick as well, with a curious hump on the front of its head. It was extraordinarily colourful for an inhabitant of muddy rivers, a mixture of red, black, blue and yellow. Bahat caught a couple of these fish among the whirlpools that form where the Bole river meets the Segama. He at once announced that he must collect fruit to make *ikan jeruk*, a sour fish preserve. He returned a few hours later with several cut lengths of bamboo six inches thick and some large sour fruit that grew in the forest. He chopped the fish into small pieces and mixed the bits with a paste of tapioca flour, salt and mashed fruits. These culinary efforts were then packed into the lengths of bamboo, and the ends sealed with the leaves of wild ginger and bound with vines. The precious preserves were stored away in the back of Bahat's hut, and it was days before I was permitted to taste this novelty. The raw, gooey results of Bahat's care looked and smelled far from promising, but I found them quite tasty, rather like a mixture of smoked salmon and anchovies.

Some of the river fish were impressively large. Bahat one day excelled himself by landing a seven-foot sawfish on a flimsy handline. Occasionally he caught vicious-tailed stingrays. I was surprised that both these relatives of the shark family could live so far from the sea. My introduction to another large fish, the fabulous, fatty *tapah*, was something of an adventure. We had eaten our evening meal and I was ready for bed when Bahat asked me if I wished to go fishing. I remonstrated about the late hour and the darkness, but he explained that night was the best time to catch the *tapah*. I agreed to go as I was intrigued by the curious rod Bahat had been making for *tapah*. It was a stout, six-foot bamboo with a strong line bound along its length. The line extended only a few inches beyond the tip of the rod and was tied to a large wicked hook. Just behind the hook was fixed a stiff cloth pad that served as a lure and in no way resembled the small fish Bahat said it represented.

I helped Bahat and Pingas untie the small *sampan* on the beach. The night was cloudy and once we rounded the first bend, which cut off the glow of our camp fire, we were in almost total darkness. Bahat sat at the front of the boat guiding us on. Mostly we crept along close under the bank, edging the wooden craft forwards by pushing against the gravel bottom with our belian wood paddles or pulling ourselves on projecting branches. After each bend of the river we had to paddle furiously to cross over to the calmer side. It was a cool, stimulating exercise, and in about half an hour we were nearly a mile upstream of our camp. We rested by the bank for a few minutes while my companions smoked cigarettes. The fragrant smoke of the nipah palm leaves in which they rolled their tobacco hung heavily in the still night air.

Eventually they were ready and we drifted slowly out into the fast currents. We glided passively back the way we had come, Pingas steering by tiny movements of the paddle he held deep in the water. In spite of the darkness the two Dusuns knew exactly where they were and what pools, rocks and tangles of dead wood lay in the river beneath us.

Bahat, in the bows, raised his *tapah* rod, then smacked it with surprising force on to the water beside me. He held the tip beneath the surface for a few moments, wiggling the cloth lure quickly up and down so that it splashed along the river's surface. He raised the rod again and repeated the procedure on the other side of the boat. He explained that the *tapah* was a large carnivorous fish that had learned how to steal smaller fish already caught on night lines. Bahat had lost several fish along this stretch of river so he knew there were *tapah* to be had. They lived in the deeper pools but would rise to investigate the splashing of his lure and, taking it for a struggling fish, would strike the hooked line.

As though to illustrate his point there was a loud splash and the bamboo was suddenly jerked into a violent U-shape. I was surprised at the power of the fish and even more surprised after a couple of exciting minutes when Bahat flashed his torchlight on to the flapping creature he had hauled in to the boat. It was a vicious looking catfish with a broad, well-whiskered head and a tapering body some four feet long. Its gaping mouth was crowded with hundreds of sharp teeth, all pointing backwards. Anything caught in that cruel mouth would edge further inside the fish's jaws with every struggle and Bahat was very cautious as he dislodged the cloth pad from this armoury.

We continued to drift effortlessly through the darkness, and it seemed no time at all before three fat *tapah* fish were wriggling worryingly close to my feet. When we reached camp, Bahat put the fish in a large cane cage he had already prepared so that they could be kept alive in the river until we should want to eat them. Over the next few days we had several wonderful meals and I had to agree with the Dusuns that *tapah* was the most delicious fish I had ever eaten.

Tapah are also palatable to monitor lizards, which will eat almost anything. Monitors have long, forked tongues like those of snakes which they flick in and out to scent the wind or the water. This device is amazingly sensitive, and it does not take them long to trace a corpse in the forest or the offal of a dismembered carcass beside the river. Monitors were abundant all along the Segama river and many grew to a good nine feet. Like shy prehistoric creatures they would creep up to feast where we had gutted fish or pigs on the beach, dragging themselves stealthily forwards, raising a long, thin head high in the air to scent the wind, then moving on again. At the slightest smell of danger they would turn and run, their bodies raised well off the ground and their tails flashing crazily from side to side.

One morning we discovered that the *tapah* cage had been broken into, and this called for a war on the monitors. Bahat and Pingas baited two lines with pig meat and left them on the beach by the river's edge. Sure enough when I got back to camp that evening the culprit had already been caught and was hanging by the fire from the roof of our camp hut. It was an enormous lizard, and in its stomach Bahat had found the remains of our last *tapah*. "Never mind," he said, "*biawak* makes a pretty good substitute." And he started to cut up the reptile for cooking.

Apart from monitors, there were a number of other animals that competed with us in fishing, including crocodiles, birds and otters. Crocodiles were not much in evidence since the nearest ones lived an hour's

Jungle shrubbery crowds to the banks of Sarawak's murky brown Rajang river, taking every possible advantage of the unobstructed light.

journey upstream in two deep pools formed where the river rounded sharp bends. We saw them from our camp only after a heavy rainstorm when the river became turbulent. Then two crocodiles were washed downstream from their pools and drifted idly past us rather than battle to retain their ground. On other occasions we were reminded of their presence by several ripped up carcasses of wild pigs floating by.

We saw much more of the birds. Fish eagles, ospreys and kites swooped to snatch fish from the water with their sharp, curved talons. Stork-billed and black-capped kingfishers sat patiently waiting for smaller fry, then dived with lightning speed to seize their prey in dagger-like bills. The snake-bird or darter earned his fish in a more energetic manner, swimming with remarkable speed beneath the water, chasing his quarry back and forth till he could lunge with his snake-like neck and spear the fish with his beak. The darter is related to the cormorants and, like them, lacks the oily waterproofing that most waterbirds have on their feathers. It is therefore deprived of buoyancy and floats with its body submerged and only its long neck and head above the surface. This lack of buoyancy makes possible its amazing sub-aquatic performances but has the disadvantage that the bird's flight feathers become water-logged. Whenever darters emerge from the water they must perch on a rock or log to dry themselves in the sunshine, with tail spread and wings comically outstretched and flapping.

These fish-eaters were all regarded as pests by the Dusuns, but none incurred the hatred that was reserved for *rongon*, the otter. A family of otters certainly provides fierce competition when it comes to catching fish, and they can tackle even large *luot* and *tapah*. Possibly the Dusuns' hatred was justified, but I had to admit that of all the riverine fauna, otters were my favourite. Occasionally otters came past our camp but usually they kept their distance, and it was only on our boating trips that we met these sleek animals with any regularity. They were wonderfully active creatures and always seemed to have time to spare for sheer enjoyment: swimming, chasing each other or sliding down the bank into the river. I was always surprised that the Dusuns were blind to the otters' engaging, blunt-nose appearance and enchanting, inquisitive playfulness. I made my men grudgingly agree that they would not kill any otters while they were in my employ.

One day when I accompanied Pingas on a trip up the Bole river in search of durian fruit, we rounded a bend and saw a family of otters cavorting beside the river on the far shore. I drew the boat back under the bank and we climbed out to watch them from behind some ferns. Slowly the otters, an adult and four playful cubs, worked their way down the beach. Their progress was slowed by a non-stop game of tag among the youngsters. When they were nearly level with us they sneaked into the river, and five black bodies bobbed up and down as they wrestled and played hide-and-seek in the brown water.

One cub swam, head raised, looking all about him to see where his submerged playmates would resurface. He turned over on his back and drifted leisurely towards us. When the other otters emerged on the far shore, the single cub climbed out on our bank and stood high on his hind legs, whistling to his family. He was no more than five yards from us and I could feel Pingas itching for action. The other otters suddenly sneaked up the far bank and into the forest. Our cub dashed to the river, slid gracefully in, swam rapidly across, and was soon racing after the rest of the family. We broke our cover and I asked Pingas if that had not been an exciting experience. "Yes," replied the unrepentant Dusun; "if I had had a stone I could have killed him."

My favourite waterways were the smaller tributaries that wind like fairyland tunnels through varied and beautiful vegetation. So long as you do not mind having your feet in the cool water for hours at a time and do not slip on the smooth stones and boulders, these afford a relatively direct and clear passage through the forest.

Bronzed and green damsel flies flit delicately from their rock perches as you advance. The occasional kingfisher shrieks with alarm and hurries on ahead, only to be disturbed again a few minutes later. Little fish shoal to and fro in the shallow pools or converge greedily on a tiny pebble thrown into the water, imagining it to be a fruit or some clumsy insect. Fresh-water terrapins scuttle away to seek shelter in the deepest corners. Sandy beaches are thrown up on the stream bends and here the tracks of forest animals tell what else has used the same easy road through the jungle: wild pigs, civets, deer, wildcats and sometimes elephants or even rhinoceros. The unhurried gurgle of water rippling over pebbles, the pendulous feathery lianas and vivid green ferns all combine to form a soothing, relaxing atmosphere.

It was along the beds of shallow streams that I met with one curious natural phenomenon for which I had no explanation. I found several beautifully rounded circles of gravel standing clear out of the water. They were like little castles about two feet in diameter, surrounded by water-filled moats where the gravel had been removed. They had surely been made by some animal but I could tell neither what creature was responsible nor what the piles might be for. I asked Bahat about them and he said he thought they were made by frogs. There were certainly many frogs living along the streams. Large ones would sometimes leap several feet to splosh into the water as I drew near, but I had never seen a frog anywhere near one of the mounds.

I wondered if perhaps frogs might have heaped gravel over their spawn to protect them and I carefully dissected a couple of hills to test this theory. I found no sign of spawn, no tadpoles, nothing. They were simply piles of gravel. Quite by accident I solved the mystery several weeks later. I had been out at night looking for nocturnal animals by torchlight and was returning home across one of the many streams. For a few moments I saw it before it leaped away; there was no mistaking it. A huge frog had been sitting on top of the pile of gravel. I suddenly realized that the piles were used only at night and that they were pulpits built by individual frogs from which to broadcast their deep, purring mating calls all the more effectively. Where the stream was rocky the frogs could climb on to suitable stones, but where there were only gravelly shallows they had to build castles.

Along the streams I also met many forest butterflies using the clear space as aerial corridors. Large *Charaxes* flitted powerfully along my path, then settled on a convenient perch while I passed beneath. On one occasion I saw the high-speed flutter of dark sickle wings as a Rajah Brooke bird-wing hovered to find a drinking place in the wet sand. Occasionally I was lucky enough to meet several of these spectacular butterflies with six-inch wingspans, sipping drunkenly from the side of a stream where mineral-rich water seeped up through the sand or where some animal had urinated. They were extracting the minerals from the tasty juices and squirting out the discarded water from their tails.

The more careful observer will notice, as Alfred Russel Wallace did when he first described this insect to science, that all the butterflies drinking in this way are males. Indeed, for many years no females were caught, and the reason is quite simple: they spend their time out of sight in the forest canopy, mating and finding suitables places to deposit their eggs. They have more important things to do than fill themselves with the rich waters of forest streams. Both sexes of this gorgeous insect have the same elegant markings, iridescent green half-crescents arranged along black velvet wings, set off by a scarlet furry collar; but the females are slightly larger and splashed with white. Wallace thought the butterfly so magnificent that he named it *Ornithoptera brookeana* after his friend, the White Rajah of Sarawak.

Other butterflies, too, come to the stream banks to sip. At certain times of year hundreds or even thousands of these pretty creatures may be packed together like a fluttering carpet, exploding into a dazzling snowstorm as you approach. Most are whites and yellows of the Pieridae family, mingled with little yellow *Eurema* butterflies and larger orange-tips. Others are purple and brown milkweeds, blue and black swallowtails, red nymphalids and tiny iridescent lycaenid blues.

I saw many butterflies along the banks of the Segama, including some of the most splendid species. Enormous black and yellow bird-wings of the genus *Troides* glided high over the river, then dived to sip nectar from the orange vine blossoms. The large spotted milkweed butterflies, *Idea*, preferred the flowerheads of the *Lantana* weeds. These extra-ordinary butterflies floated in the wind like the winged seeds of one of the large forest vines. The local people called them *kupu-kupu kertas* or paper butterflies on account of their papery, semi-transparent wings. Blue and green *Graphium* species flitted along the waterline while the more fragile *Papilio* butterflies settled to feed on the plume-like flowers of *Eugenia* bushes. Here the swallowtails competed for nectar with glossy-feathered sun-birds, huge black and yellow carpenter bees and shimmering green wood beetles.

The swallowtails were Wallace's favourite family of butterflies and although beetles remained his first love, he made a large collection of these and other types. Forty-two years after Wallace did his collecting in Sarawak, another professional entomologist arrived in Borneo from England to take up the curatorship of the Sarawak museum. Robert Shelford also was an evolutionist and his collecting and careful observations of insects helped him to clarify current ideas about adaptive coloration, of great importance to our understanding of the mechanism of evolution. I too kept a butterfly net and started to make my own modest collection. To the Dusuns I must have seemed a ludicrous figure running along the beach cursing the escaping insects, but I was fortified by the knowledge that better men than I had chased butterflies along Borneo's rivers, and to good purpose.

The Lure of Borneo

Borneo was known to Europeans for four and a half centuries, but over much of that period the island remained an enigma, a far-off paradise of sumptuous palaces, gold, sago, pepper and many exotic goods that could be bought and traded. Until recent times the great forests remained unexplored, their plants and animals still to be studied.

Europe's first substantial glimpse of Borneo was provided by the major geographical work on the East Indies in the 16th Century, *The Itinerario or Seavoyage of Jan Huygen van Linschoten to the East or Portuguese Indies*. It was published in Dutch in 1596, nearly a century after the first Europeans had set foot in Borneo. Van Linschoten had never been farther east than Goa, so his information was necessarily somewhat fanciful. He based his account on contemporary Portuguese writings and on reports from travellers to the East Indies.

In the 17th Century Dutch navigators began to produce elementary maps of Borneo like the one on the right. But the island's lack of harbours, dense jungle and fierce Dyak tribesmen kept information to a bare minimum. One of the earliest Englishmen to provide first-hand evidence, Captain Daniel Beeckman, described a skirmish with some of the Dyaks in 1718. "Even in their retreat," he wrote, "they ceased not to let fly their arrows at us, after the maner of the antient Parthians."

Only in the mid-19th Century, as British and Dutch control over Borneo became secure, did accounts of the forested interior appear. These came initially from colonial officials and servicemen and later from professional scientists like the Swede, Carl Bock, and the great English naturalist, Alfred Russel Wallace.

One of these professionals was John Whitehead, a British ornithologist who typified the passionate collector. In 1885, he described how he took "a most careful pot-shot" at a pitta, one of the multi-coloured jungle birds. Failing to find it, he was about to return to camp empty-handed when he saw "this gem of a bird creation on its back. I sat down and stroked it . . . and gazed upon one of the most lovely Eastern birds —satisfied with all the world."

One of the earliest maps of Borneo is this one, published in 1601. It was drawn by Olivier van Noort, the first Dutchman to circumnavigate the globe. The interior of the island is pure conjecture, and detailed information is restricted to the coastal areas, where van Noort has given several place names and drawn his ship resting in harbour.

BORNEO

tialis.

Cabura

Puerte Aror
Paco

Cala ndua

Rio Tamampuro

Rio Succadano Ada. manfn habet

Cota baran nin

casa

Borneo

INSULA

Equinoc,

miaõ baiao

R. de Buvulo

Malano

Laue

Puchauaraon

Bandermach ri

Tamenacevim

Ta manatos

Hermata

A symbolic plantation included coconuts (Coco), betel nuts (Arecca al Faufel) and bananas (labelled as Vyghe boomen, or fig trees).

Traders' Bonanza

The earliest ideas that 16th-Century Europe had of Borneo were built up around general and often idealized accounts of the East Indies in van Linschoten's *Itinerario*. The chronicle contained 36 plates of which several, including the two illustrated here, provided a wealth of detail about the kinds of commercially usable trees and plants. Most of the drawings were fairly accurate, but van Linschoten confused bananas with figs and showed them growing down instead of upwards.

Three of the cultivable wild plants that van Linschoten drew were the bamboo plant (left), the banyan tree with its net of aerial roots (centre) and the durian tree which produces a spiney fruit between nine inches and a foot long.

THE ORAN = OOTAN

Primates as Pets

Early visitors to Borneo were fascinated by the island's orang-utans and proboscis monkeys, mainly because of their marked resemblance to human beings.

During his visit in 1718, Captain Daniel Beeckman was so intrigued by one baby orang that he bought it for six Spanish dollars and took it aboard his ship. He noted in his diary that it was "a great thief, and loved strong liquors; for if our backs were turned, he would be at the punch bowl, and very often would open the brandy-case, take out a bottle, drink plentifully, and put it very carefully into its place again."

In 1848, midshipman Frank Marryat, whose father wrote the popular children's book, *Masterman Ready*, was much taken with what he considered to be "the scarcest monkey in Borneo . . . the proboscis". And in 1856 Alfred Russel Wallace also fell for the higher primates. He adopted a young orang which "seemed quite strong and active" and, if fed tasteless food, "would set up a scream and kick about violently, exactly like a baby in a passion".

Captain Beeckman drew a stylized portrait of the orang-utan which resembled man more than ape and reflected local attitudes towards the ape. "The natives," he wrote, "do really believe that these were formerly men, but metamorphosed into beasts for their blasphemy."

This wiry proboscis monkey, extending its arm as if in greeting, was drawn by Frank Marryat who described it as "male, very young, and with the nose more or less prominent, and giving its face a more actual resemblance to that of a man's than I had ever before seen".

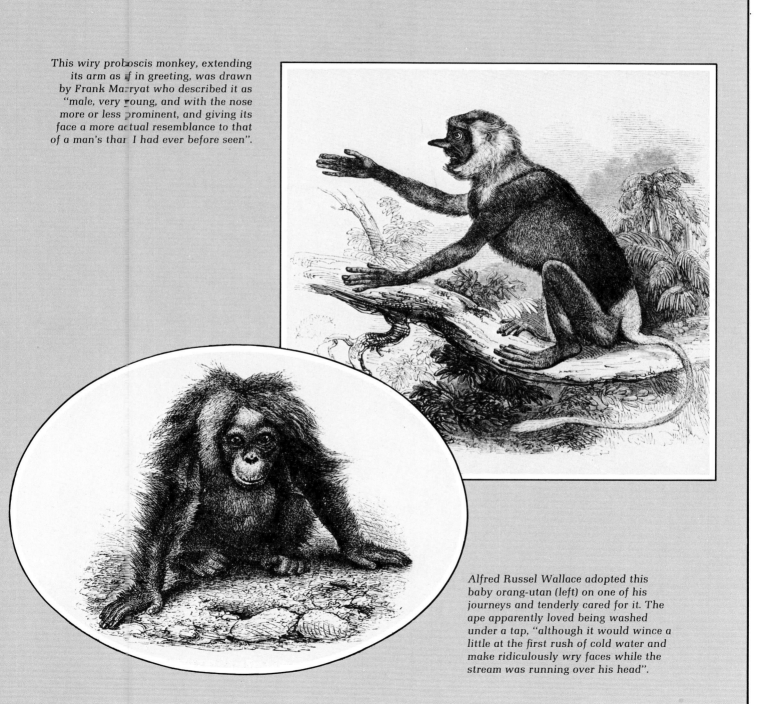

Alfred Russel Wallace adopted this baby orang-utan (left) on one of his journeys and tenderly cared for it. The ape apparently loved being washed under a tap, "although it would wince a little at the first rush of cold water and make ridiculously wry faces while the stream was running over his head".

Whitehead's catches included a munia (top), a flycatcher-warbler (middle) and a minla.

Creatures New to Science

Many 19th-Century naturalists made a point of climbing Mount Kinabalu, which soon became famous for the outstanding variety of its wildlife. The ornithologist John Whitehead was no exception. When he first visited the mountain in 1887, it had already been explored by botanists, but "for the zoologist", Whitehead wrote, "it was as yet a virgin field". On this first visit he proudly recorded having collected "some 300 birds, eighteen of which were new to science". He made smaller collections of reptiles and insects, many of which were also new, and wrote up his finds in his book *The Exploration of Mount Kina Balu*, from which these illustrations were taken.

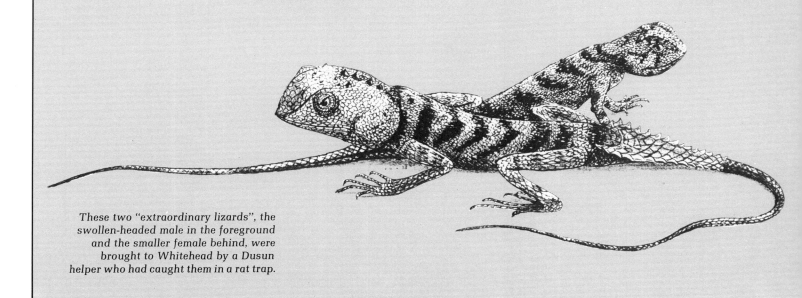

These two "extraordinary lizards", the swollen-headed male in the foreground and the smaller female behind, were brought to Whitehead by a Dusun helper who had caught them in a rat trap.

"One very handsome species" in Whitehead's butterfly collection was this pale swallowtail, which he drew from two angles.

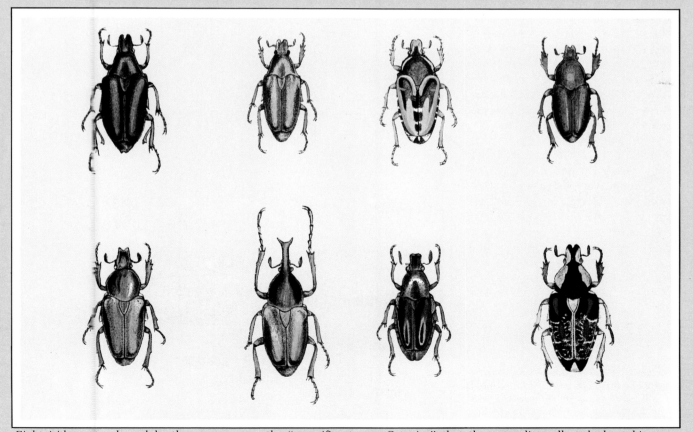

Eight iridescent coloured beetles were among the "magnificent new Cetonias" that the naturalist collected about his camp.

A Search for Head-Hunters

Jungle travelling was a hazardous experience, then as now. One hair-raising expedition, in search of the wild forest peoples, took place in 1878 when the Swedish ethnographer Carl Bock made a 700-mile journey, travelling mainly by river "through several dangerous and troublesome Dyak tribes".

His first tormentors were not the head-hunters he had been led to expect but the voracious mosquitoes which, he wryly noted, "did not get a feast of white man's blood every day". When rapids made canoeing impossible he had to march through the jungle, and this involved crossing some large rivers. He did so by means of felled trees or slender bamboo bridges on which an anxious Bock would "sway to and fro in the centre in such a manner as to induce sea-sickness and giddiness".

Finally he met the chief of the "cannibal Dyaks", a man who, as Bock wrote with pardonable hyperbole, "had fresh upon his head the blood of no less than seventy victims . . . just slaughtered and whose hands and brains he had eaten."

One of Carl Bock's detailed sketches shows him and his heavily-burdened "coolies" crossing the rapid Benangan river by means of a large tree trunk which had been "felled for the purpose".

8/ In the Limestone Caves

*The end of this rent we were unable to see in the darkness,
and a stone tossed in might be heard falling some distance
into the bowels of the hill. Small Swifts flew about in this
gloomy place of theirs and into the vaults below the rocks on
which we stood.* JOHN WHITEHEAD/ *THE EXPLORATION OF MOUNT KINA BALU*

I was returning upstream one day to my camp on the Segama river. Bahat was at the helm of our small sampan, and the outboard motor droned monotonously as he followed the twisting course of the river, weaving in and out among the shallows. Suddenly, round a sharp bend, we came face to face with a towering white cliff that rose sheer and majestic for over 400 feet. The limestone face was pocked with hundreds of tiny caves. Here and there dark blotches betrayed where bees had suspended their pendulous combs from rocky overhangs. A small fig tree clung tenaciously to the steep scarp, its twisted roots firmly secured in a narrow fissure, and lianas hung down like sweeping drapes from the clifftop. Near the base, a single large socket gaped darkly— the entrance to the Tapadong cave.

This cave had intrigued me ever since my first sight of it on my original journey upriver, and now I decided to stop for a while and investigate its hidden recesses.

The Dusuns tell of days long past when the river passage in front of the cave was guarded by a huge eagle, the Garuda, and a giant crocodile, Tarongari, which preyed on unwary travellers. Unable to pass, the Dusuns devised a plan to rid themselves of the two monsters. They launched a raft baited with meat which had been cunningly armed with bamboo spears. When the Garuda attacked the raft, it impaled itself on the sharp-pointed weapons. The injured bird managed to escape to its eyrie and then flew to another land, but in its struggles to get airborne again it dislodged two enormous boulders that crashed down, killing the crocodile below. The two rocks that are supposed to have struck the fatal blows still lie like bold sentinels beside the murky river. It was here that we moored our boat and scrambled over a scree of fallen stones and up to the entrance of the cave.

Tapadong was formed, like the many other limestone caves in Borneo, when a great outcrop of limestone was exposed to the elements. Falling rain dissolved the calcium carbonate of the limestone and ate away at fissures in the rock. Along the Baram and Mahakam rivers such erosion created no more than slits in the ground, so inconspicuous that an occasional pig or deer falls to its death down one of the narrow shafts. Elsewhere the rain excavated deep channels and holes down which it vanished, carving out subterranean halls and galleries before emerging as streamlets at what became the mouths of caves. Tapadong, Gomanton nearby, and the famous Niah caves in Sarawak have wide conspicuous entrances leading into enormous chambers. In the spectacular Great Cave of Niah, for example, the main chamber inside the mouth is 800 feet wide and more than 200 feet high.

All the large caves offer a dark and relatively safe refuge from the surrounding rain-drenched forest. Great numbers of tiny swiftlets and bats roost and breed deep within the rocky galleries, and other animals like civets, snakes, lizards and porcupines sometimes venture inside. In the distant past the caves provided homes and burial places for peoples whose relics have been found at Tapadong and also in special profusion at Niah. For many years the caves have been important sources of the edible swiftlets' nests, and of bat and swiftlet guano, which is collected in large quantities for use as fertilizer. Although no one lives in the caves nowadays, some of them are still used by the forest peoples as burial places.

As we entered the Tapadong cave a two-way stream of swiftlets swirled over our heads, bustling noisily in and out of the shadows. Moving deeper into the chamber we left the last shafts of daylight behind and had to resort to torches to find our way. Weird buttresses of carved rock, stalagmites and dripping stalactites made the cavern look like a satanic sepulchre. Armies of bats twittered in the domes above us; we picked them out in the beams of our torches.

The largest numbers of swiftlets and bats are found in the blackest recesses of the caves. The reason for their success in exploiting this midnight habitat is that they can find their way in the darkness. Their secret is echo-location or sonar. The principle is quite simple, and we all use it instinctively on occasion. If you wake up at night in a strange room and make a noise, it is possible from the resonance of the sound to get some idea of the size of the room. In their systematic echo-location, birds and bats utter a succession of brief sounds and monitor the echoes. The bats use ultrasonic frequencies, those beyond the range of human hearing, but the swiftlets send out a series of clearly audible clicks—about six a second—which create a curious rattling noise.

There were quite a number of swiftlets in the Tapadong cave at that moment, each one sending out its rattling clicks. When the colony was here in force the din would be deafening and I wondered how on earth each bird could distinguish its own rebounding call from the rest. An equally baffling problem arises from the fact that swiftlets fly very fast and must therefore interpret and act upon their echoes virtually instantaneously. Considering the technical difficulties, it seemed miraculous that some hideous multiple collisions did not occur.

Swiftlets use their sonar principally for finding their way through the dark galleries to their roosts. As soon as they settle on their nests, they switch it off. They do the same when they go out during the day to hunt insects. When departing, a noisy stream of birds will fall magically silent as they cross the demarcation line between darkness and daylight. Often they make extra use of their sonar by setting off before dawn and returning after dark, which enables them to hunt over wider areas and to take advantage of the swarms of flying ants that emerge with the dusk. But they do most of their hunting by day with their perfectly adequate eyesight.

Bats, on the other hand, hunt at night and need a far more sophisticated sonar system for the purpose. Whereas swiftlets use frequencies generally between 1.5 and 5.5 kilocycles a second, bats operate on much higher frequencies. Some species of cave-dwelling bats emit this ultrasonic sound from their nostrils, and have evolved elaborately shaped noses and ears. The horseshoe bats, for instance, have large mobile ears and elaborate structures of skin on their snouts called nose-leaves with which they can make their signals directional, spreading them over a wide arc or focusing them into a narrow beam to penetrate a greater distance. The incredible accuracy of the bats' sonar allows them to hunt tiny flying insects in total darkness.

Bats and swiftlets make good neighbours. Their habits are conveniently complementary. Each group uses a separate part of the roof, so there is little dispute over roosting space. Nor are they in direct compe-

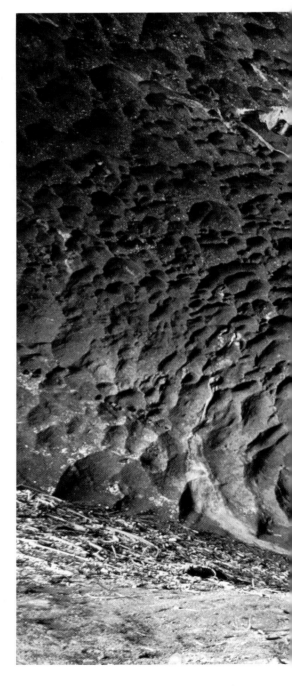

Glistening limestone sculpted ages ago by subterranean water forms the roof of the Gomanton cave in north Sabah. Bat guano litters the floor.

tition for food: the insects the swiftlets find by day are different from those hunted by bats at night. Even the traffic system at the cave mouth is organized to avoid mutual interference. In the same way that aeroplanes have flight paths to avoid collisions, so bats streaming out of the cave in the evening keep to one corner of the wide entrance, leaving the rest of the mouth free for the returning swiftlets. Most of the bats are back in the cave before the swiftlets flood out on their dawn exodus.

The rattling din of flying swiftlets continued as we picked our way cautiously along one of the tunnels that radiated from the main cave. Now and then we paused to examine the swiftlet nests festooning the walls beside us. Whereas young bats are left hanging from bare ledges while their parents go out to search for food, young swiftlets are provided with more permanent homes—rubbery, cup-shaped nests stuck to the walls or ceiling of the cave. These tiny platforms are only a couple of inches long and seem the most precarious support for hatched nestlings and adults alike. It is scarcely surprising that no swiftlets lay more than two eggs at a time, while some lay only one egg.

What is surprising is that anyone should have been smitten with the idea that these swiftlet nests would make marvellous soup. They are singularly unpleasant objects, soiled with droppings, mixed with bedraggled feathers and crawling with parasitic bugs and other insects. Yet the culinary demand for this gelatinous delicacy was drawing Chinese traders to Borneo 1,200 years ago, during the T'ang dynasty, and the trade still flourishes today. Most of the nests used in the soup-making process—because they are the most readily available—are the so-called black nests of the Low's swiftlet, the second largest of the five swiftlet species in Borneo. Much more valuable are the so-called white nests of the brown-rumped swiftlets that build in the smaller galleries. The composition of the white nest is mainly saliva mixed with a few breast feathers. The saliva, secreted as a gummy fluid from a gland in the bird's throat, solidifies into a rubbery substance when it comes into contact with the air. The nests are never served by themselves, for the odd fact is that this delicacy is virtually tasteless—provided, of course, that it has been properly cleaned.

The methods employed to gather nests from the ceilings vary from cave to cave. In these Tapadong galleries, which are relatively low and small, all the collector needs is a rake-like tool with a long handle, together with daring and agility. In the Niah caves, on the other hand, nest collecting techniques are both dangerous and spectacular. Tall masts, or *tiang*, are built of bamboo sections, one slotting into another

Near the mouth of a cave, a white-bellied swiftlet appears too big for its nest of moss, grass and lichen fastened to the rock wall. But in fact the small size of the nest enables the weak-legged bird to become airborne with minimum effort. All it has to do is roll over sideways and, as it drops, spread its long wings.

until the roof comes within reach, and then guyed with rattan ropes. These precarious, swaying constructions are safe only for a couple of years or so and then have to be replaced. A more permanent type of *tiang* is made of belian-wood poles pegged together and hung from cross-bars wedged in the roof, and these may last for decades.

The nester climbs the *tiang* by using a cloth tied to both feet across the insteps. The cloth helps him grip the bamboo. Sometimes he scorns even this. The strength needed for the job is tremendous and once a man has left the ground he is completely beyond the range of help. Should his arms or legs weaken or become affected by cramp, the only way he is likely to get relief is to spread his knees so that the soles of his tied feet are pressed flat on the pole.

Having finally reached the top, the collector or *tukang julok* scrapes off the nests with a wavering bamboo pole, up to 40 feet long, made of jointed sections. At the far end it bears an iron blade, rather like a hoe, and a lighted beeswax candle to illuminate the proceedings. The nests and their contents fall to the floor where the collector's assistant, or *tukang pungut*, can gather them up.

Looking at a ravaged cave in the aftermath of a collection one wonders how the swiftlet colonies can possibly survive such regular and whole-sale devastation. Whatever their secret, the birds have plainly managed to maintain themselves in spite of centuries of interference. From the few statistics which exist of past seasons it seems that the colonies fluctuate in size, but it may well be that the changes are not due to man, because similar variations occur in caves that are not harvested. Some outside factor, such as food supply, could be the cause. Certainly the Tapadong swiftlets did not appear to have suffered from the collectors' activities. I noticed that only a few of the nests we were examining contained eggs, and Bahat explained that nearly all of them were newly built. Only a few weeks before, the cave had been virtually stripped of nests by the local people and the empty ones we saw now represented the birds' second attempt at breeding this year.

We had now penetrated into the deepest recesses of the Tapadong cave and the air had grown hot and stifling from the body heat of the bats and swiftlets living here. Our worst problem was the amount of waste created by these large subterranean colonies. The quantity of food collected from the forest by their combined forces defies belief. As soon as one starts multiplying by several million the few grammes that an individual might catch in several hours' hunting, gigantic statistics begin to emerge. One zoologist has calculated that the main cave at Niah, for example, contains some 300,000 bats and two million swiftlets, and that between them they must catch every 24 hours between six and seven tons of insects. Much of the nourishment is absorbed in their digestive systems, of course, but there is enough waste matter dropped on to the floor to make walking under one of these colonies very unpleasant.

We were slithering over a thick carpet of slimy guano from which rose a pungent smell of ammonia. The guano is rich in nitrogen and is highly prized by the Bornean people as a fertilizer for their hillside fields of pepper. But these great mounds of excrement also form the basis for a series of weird food chains. A host of foul scavengers exists to exploit any leftovers. When I played the beam of my torch on the ground, I could see that the guano was shimmering with cockroaches, packed two or three thousand to the square yard. These marauding insects feast on the dead and dying creatures that fall from the crowded roof: eggs, nestlings, stricken bats, all are devoured. In a population of millions, every hour has its corpses, and black darkling beetles shuffle like sinister undertakers through the seething mass, speedily carting away and consuming any dead cockroaches they find. Snakes and rats make occasional visits into the dark interior to exploit the regular harvest of decaying matter. Centipedes lurk in the shadowy crevices to pounce on any overspill of wandering insects, and their long feeler legs keep them raised above the slimy guano. Their bite is poisonous and the knowledge of their hidden presence made me extremely cautious about where I put my hands in the darkness.

There are many other ingenious or unpleasant specializations for cave existence. Cave crickets no more than two inches long with immense antennae pose a great problem to the swiftlets. Although the cave roof and walls are inaccessible to most predators, this cricket can walk freely over the rocky walls, seeking out and devouring young nestlings with its strong jaws, and biting through shells to feast on the yolks of unattended eggs. Then there is a moth whose larvae share with the Chinese a taste for the saliva nests. If too many grubs attack the same nest it eventually collapses, spilling out its contents, whether eggs or nestlings, for the waiting scavengers below.

Perhaps the most amazing of the cave dwellers is the hairy earwig. At the Niah cave this peculiar creature was discovered to have colonized one particular spot. Year after year the insect is found in exactly the same place in the cave, and the Sarawak Museum has proudly declared this the world's first hairy earwig sanctuary.

A naked bulldog bat, hanging from a branch inside a cave mouth (above), displays its free-standing tail, clinging toes and two thumb claws. This species of bat has a pig-like face (below) and thick folds of oily, flaking skin where parasitical earwigs nestle and feed.

Hairy earwigs have been found in other caves but always in very localized patches. All their haunts have one thing in common—they lie directly below the roosts of certain species of bat, especially an ugly, furless creature known as the naked bulldog bat. The hairy earwigs alone among the cave scavengers seem able to deal with the evil smelling droppings and occasional corpses of this grotesque species. Yet another type of hairy earwig spends much of its time as a huge ectoparasite on the same bat, living on the wrinkled body and feeding on its oily skin. Other warm blooded vertebrates of the caves also have their share of parasites, but none are so large or anything like as loathsome as the earwigs that cling to the naked bat.

I had seen enough for one day and I was glad to get back to the cave mouth where the air was fresh and the only reminder of the ecosystem within was the midday trickle of swiftlets leaving or entering the cave.

For thousands of years the mouths of caves were the homes of pre-historic man. Standing at the entrance to the Tapadong, I could imagine how reassuring it must have been to have a roof over your head which could not be blown down in one of the violent forest storms nor pene-trated by the monsoon rains. Much has been discovered about how these early men lived, what they ate, what tools they used and how they treated their dead. Preliminary excavations at Tapadong have un-earthed many relics of long human habitation. Stone adzes, shell kitchen-middens and even an early bronze axe-head were found here. More has been learnt about Borneo's early man in other caves. In 1954, Tom and Barbara Harrisson began a series of excavations in the Great Cave at Niah. Even before completion of the first trial trench, it was clear that this was going to be one of the most important archaeological sites in South-East Asia, with remains of human habitation going back to Middle Palaeolithic times, 50,000 years ago.

Bones of prehistoric man were found in the lower strata together with an assortment of crude stone tools and the bones of large animals: pigs, deer, rhinoceroses, an extinct form of giant pangolin, monkeys and even orang-utans. Clear plastic covers were erected to preserve *in situ* the crouched remains of early burials exactly as they were unearthed by careful archaeologists. Higher layers gave an interesting record of how tool design and the proportions of different animals in the diet had changed during the Mesolithic period.

By Neolithic times, 5,000 years ago, man was no longer living in the caves. He built rough shelters in the forest much as the Punans do today. The caves were then used only for burials, each corpse being provided with beautifully polished stone adzes and colourful pottery for use in the after-life. Traces of bamboo, nets and decorative necklaces of hornbill bones and the beaks of bee-eaters were also found.

One of the most exciting discoveries at Niah was a small subsidiary cave that had been overlooked by previous investigators. Inside, the walls were decorated with bold red paintings of birds, boats and prancing figures. Rows of wooden boat-shaped coffins pointed into the centre of the cavern and the dusty floor around these "ships of the dead" was strewn with bones. This was a direct link between past and present, for the Njadju people of south-east Kalimantan still practise a "ship of the dead" cult and their art and folklore tie up closely with the scenes in Niah's painted cave. Elements of Punan traditions, too, can be traced far back into the archaeological past, and cave burials are still the common practice in several parts of Borneo, including the area around my Segama river camp.

Some time after my visit to the Tapadong cave, an elderly cousin of Bahat's died and I had the honour of joining an all-male burial party that accompanied the woman's body to its final resting place, a small cave named Batu Balus which is set back from the Segama river on the opposite bank to the Tapadong cave, and about half a mile downstream. Here, for the last 700 years, the Segama Dusuns have brought their dead. Our party paddled upriver from Bahat's *kampong*, leaving the wailing womenfolk behind. As the bereaved sons shouldered the coffin and bore it in silence up the steep hillside, the doleful beat of a great bronze gong echoed around the rocky cliffs. The coffin was exceedingly heavy, being carved from a generous length of hard merbau wood, and it was wrapped in colourful cloth bound in traditional patterns with strips of split rattan cane.

The funeral procession wound its way to the foot of the cliff and there, halfway up the face, I could see the dark mouth of the burial cave. Coloured flags hung limply from bamboo poles to frighten away any unwelcome spirits. A huge ladder of cut saplings stretched to the cave and it was up this creaking structure that the heavy coffin was now hauled. Steadied by willing hands and shoulders, pulled with two strong rattan ropes, the coffin rose steadily rung by rung until it finally reached the shadowy entrance where it was gently carried to its appointed position in the cave.

The rest of us followed. The air inside was still and cold, and foul with the smell of decay. It was not difficult to believe that the gloomy cavern was haunted by wandering spirits. This was no place for the living: there were no swiftlets and few bats. The beam of my torch fell on the stacks of coffins. There were hundreds and hundreds of them from generations long past, neatly piled against the wall of the cave. The more recent coffins were still in good order but those at the bottom of the stack were crumbling with age, and dry powdery dust covered the floor. Here and there yellow bones and a grinning skull protruded from the rotting pile. I paused to examine some of the exquisitely carved belian-wood boat paddles, decorated knife handles and ancient Chinese bowls and jars that had been left for the use of the spirits of the dead.

The burial service itself was brief. An old man mumbled some ancient prayers, beseeching the corpse to remain content and not to come back to haunt the villagers. He erected a parasol above the coffin, smote it with a rattan rod and sprinkled it with rice. With these rites over, we withdrew and made our way back to the waiting boats, each member of the party plucking a spray of green leaves along the way, a symbol of rebirth with which to greet the rest of the village. Somehow, having participated in this age-old Dusun ceremony, I felt I had established a link with the past, a link through thousands of years of cave burials with those first men who lived in Borneo and with those crouched skeletons in the lowest levels at the Niah cave. I shared a knowledge of the primeval rain forest in which they hunted, of plants and animals now extinct, and yet others that still survive. But even now the timber companies were moving closer and I knew that all this would soon be destroyed by their advance, and that one more point of contact with our past would be severed.

The Tranquil World of Leaves

Wandering through the great forests of Borneo, you will often see very little but leaves. There are leaves in the ground litter, high in the canopy, festooning the branches and trunks of the forest giants.

So many leaves *en masse* might seem monotonous, and at first glance many of them do in fact look much alike: dark green, hard and shiny, often with long tips. But when you live in the forest, you become aware of the innumerable variations of design, texture and colour, especially where sunlight breaks through. A few striking examples have been captured in these photographs.

Every shape and colour is intimately related to the plant's lifestyle in the forest. The long tips help water to drip off quickly after the frequent tropical downpours, and the waxy skins, or cuticles, keep the leaves from becoming sodden and so protect them from attack by fungi. In the hot, dry atmosphere of the canopy, the cuticles fulfil a valuable service in cutting down evaporation from within the plant.

The colours vary according to the leaves' age, their position in shade or sunlight, and their species. The main colour ingredient is chlorophyll, the green pigment that converts sunlight into energy. Blue, orange and yellow pigments also exist in smaller quantities, and the varying proportions of all these create an infinite range of shades.

Inside the forest, the leaves are generally dark, because rain-forest plants are highly efficient chlorophyll producers and generate large amounts in spite of the gloom. But there are exceptions. You can often see newly formed leaves hanging limply red, white or even bluish before the chlorophyll builds up. Some maverick plants seem to flourish with comparatively little chlorophyll, displaying the lack of pigment with lighter shades of green.

Out in the open grow other plants which could not survive in the darkness of the forest. Many have pale, fresh-looking leaves, and the secondary pigments are much in evidence. When you look at the delicately coloured *Bryophyllum*, for example, its leaves seem almost blue until the sun dapples them and reassures your visual preconceptions that they are green. Everywhere, the play of light and shade, falling dimly upon dull, opaque foliage or shining through translucent ferns, creates a world of peace and tranquillity, somewhere man can be at ease.

A FERN FROND ABOUT TO UNFURL ITS LEAFLETS

A FAN-SHAPED ALOCASIA MACRORHIZA LEAF

FERN FROND SPOTTED WITH SPORE CASES

A GLEICHENIA FERN BRANCHING INTO NEW STEMS

LIMP YOUNG LEAVES WITH DRIP TIPS

A BRILLIANT SEALING WAX PALM

SUN-DAPPLED LEAVES OF BRYOPHYLLUM

Bibliography

Attenborough, David, *Zoo Quest for a Dragon*. Lutterworth, 1957.

Beccari, Odoardo, *Wanderings in the Great Forests of Borneo*. Translated from the Italian by Enrico H. Giglioli and edited by F. H. H. Guillemard. Archibald Constable & Co. Ltd., 1904.

Burbidge, F. W., *Gardens of the Sun*. John Murray, 1880.

Dwight Davis, D., "Mammals of the Lowland Rain-Forest of North Borneo", *Bulletin of the National Museum of the State of Singapore*. No. 31, 1962.

Freeman, J. D., "Iban Augury" in *The Birds of Borneo* by Bertram E. Smythies. Oliver and Boyd, 1960, pp. 73-98.

Fuente, Felix Rodriguez de la, *World of Wildlife*, Vol. 7. Orbis Publishing Ltd., 1971-73.

Harrison, John, *Mammals of Sabah*. The Sabah Society, 1964.

Harrisson, Barbara, *Orang-utan*. Collins, 1962.

Harrisson, Tom, Ed., *Borneo Jungle*. Lindsay Drummond Ltd., 1938.

Harrisson, Tom, "Birds and Men in Borneo", in *The Birds of Borneo*, Bertram E. Smythies. Oliver and Boyd, 1960, pp. 20-61.

Hatton, Frank, *North Borneo*. Sampson Low, Marston, Searle, & Rivington, 1885.

Hervey, G. F., and Hems, J., *Freshwater Tropical Aquarium Fishes*. Batchworth Press, 1962.

Huxley, Julian, *Ants*. Arrow Books, 1962 (first published in 1930).

Kyle, Harry M., *The Biology of Fishes*. Sidgwick & Jackson, Ltd., 1926.

Low, Hugh, *Sarawak*. Richard Bentley, 1848.

MacDonald, Malcolm, *Borneo People*. Jonathan Cape, 1956.

McElroy, W. D., and Seliger, Howard H., "Biological Luminescence" in *Scientific American*, Dec., 1962.

MacKinnon, John, *In Search of the Red Ape*. Collins, 1974.

Marshall, N. B., *The Life of Fishes*. Weidenfeld and Nicolson, 1965.

Medway, Lord, *Mammals of Borneo*. Malaysian Branch of the Royal Asiatic Society, 1965.

Medway, Lord, "Cave Swiftlets" in *The Birds of Borneo* by Bertram E. Smythies. Oliver and Boyd, 1960, pp. 62-72.

Polunin, Ivan T., "Who Says Fish Can't Climb Trees?" *National Geographic*, Vol. 141, No. 1, 1972; pp. 85-91.

Richards, P. W., *The Life of the Jungle*. McGraw-Hill Book Co., 1970.

Richards, P. W., *The Tropical Rain Forest*. Cambridge University Press, Fifth Impression, 1974.

Runciman, Steven, *The White Rajahs*. Cambridge University Press, 1960.

Sanderson, Ivan T., *Living Mammals of the World*. Hamish Hamilton, 1969.

The Sarawak museum journal. Kuching Museum, Sarawak. Vols 1-20.

Savonius, Moira, *Mushrooms and Fungi*. Octopus Books, 1974.

Shelford, Robert W. C., *A Naturalist in Borneo*. T. Fisher Unwin Ltd., 1916.

Smythies, Bertram E., *The Birds of Borneo*. Oliver and Boyd, 1960.

Sterba, Gunther, *Freshwater Fishes of the World*. Translated and revised by Denys Tucker, Studio Vista, 1967.

St. John, Spenser, *Life in the Forests of the Far East*. (2 vols.). Smith, Elder, and Co., 1862.

Wallace, Alfred Russel, *The Malay Archipelago*. Macmillan, 1898.

Wallace, Alfred Russel, *My Life*. Chapman and Hall Ltd., 1908.

Zahl, Paul A., "The Secrets of Nature's Night Lights", *National Geographic*, Vol. 140, No. 1, 1971; pp. 45-69.

Acknowledgements

The author and editors of this book wish to thank the following: Ian Bishop, Natural History Museum, London; Richard Brock, BBC Natural History Unit; Brunei Museum, Brunei; Ellen Brush, London; Mike Callaghan, Kalimantan; Peter Cockburn, Sabah; Charles Dettmer, Thames Ditton, Surrey; A. G. C. Grandison, Natural History Museum, London; Allen Henry, Kalimantan; Professor R. Holtum, Royal Botanical Gardens, Kew; David Jenkins, Park Warden, Kinabalu National Park, Kota Kinabalu; Kuching Museum, Kuching; Tony Lamb, Sabah; Alan and Dorothy Logan, Banggi Island, Sabah; Tony Long, Brede, Sussex; Malaysian Airline Systems; David McCredie, Sabah; Lord Medway, Saxmundham, Suffolk; Dr. Ivan Polunin, Singapore; Dr. Derek Reid, Royal Botanical Gardens, Kew; Mr. and Mrs. Riggenbach, Kayan River, Kalimantan; Sabah District Office; Sabah Forestry Department; Sabah Land Development Board; Ken Scriven, World Wildlife Fund, Kuala Lumpur; Stanley de Silva, Chief Game Warden, Sabah.

Picture Credits

Sources for pictures in this book are separated from left to right by commas, from top to bottom by dashes.

Cover–Dr. Ivan Polunin. Front end papers 1, 2–Bill and Claire Leimbach. Front end paper 3, pages 1 to 5–Bill and Claire Leimbach. 6, 7–J. Alex Langley. 8, 9–Dr. Ivan Polunin. 14, 15–Map by Hunting Surveys Ltd., London. 19–By courtesy of the Forestry Department, Sarawak. 23–Dr. Ding Hou. 25–Dr. Ding Hou, Dr. J. A. R. Anderson–Dr. J. A. R. Anderson. 29–By courtesy of the Borneo Air Force, Sarawak. 33–Dr. Ivan Polunin. 34–Dr. J. A. R. Anderson. 35–Dr. Ivan Polunin. 36 to 38–Bill and Claire Leimbach. 39–Dr. Ding Hou. 43–S. C. Bisserôt. 46, 47–Dr. Ivan Polunin. 51–Bill and Claire Leimbach. 54–Tony Lamb. 58, 59–John MacKinnon. 63–Bill and Claire Leimbach. 64–C. J. Pruett from Natural Science Photos, London–C. J. Pruett from Natural Science Photos–M. P. L. Fogden. 65–C. J. Pruett from Natural Science Photos. 66 to 71–M. P. L. Fogden. 77– Dr. Ivan Polunin. 79–Lim Boo Liat. 87 to 89–John MacKinnon. 94 to 105–Bill and Claire Leimbach. 107–David Attenborough. 111–Victor Englebert from Susan Griggs Agency, London. 115–John MacKinnon. 120 to 138–Dr. Ivan Polunin. 139–J. P. Ferrero from Pitch (Paris). 145– Bill and Claire Leimbach. 150 to 159–By courtesy of the David Attenborough Collection. 163–Bill and Claire Leimbach. 164–S. C. Bisserôt. 166–Lim Boo Liat–S. C. Bisserôt. 171 to 175–Bill and Claire Leimbach. 176–Dr. Ivan Polunin. 177 to 179–Bill and Claire Leimbach.

Index

Colour reproduction by P.D.I. Ltd., Leeds, England—a Time Inc. subsidiary.
Filmsetting by C. E. Dawkins (Typesetters) Ltd., London, SE1 1UN.
Printed and bound in Belgium by Brepols S.A.—Turnhout.